AF538451

The Implementation Gap

The Implementation Gap

UNDERSTANDING REFORM IN HIGH SCHOOLS

Edited by Jonathan A. Supovitz and Elliot H. Weinbaum

FOREWORD BY MICHAEL FULLAN

Teachers College, Columbia University
New York and London

Published by Teachers College Press, 1234 Amsterdam Avenue, New York, NY 10027

Library of Congress Cataloging-in-Publication Data

The implementation gap : understanding reform in high schools / edited by Jonathan A. Supovitz and Elliot H. Weinbaum ; foreword by Michael Fullan.
p. cm.
Includes bibliographical references and index.
ISBN 978-8077-4845-9 (cloth : alk. paper)
1. Education, Secondary—United States. 2. Educational change—United States. I. Supovitz, Jonathan A. II. Weinbaum, Elliot H.

LA222.I47 2008
373.12'070973—dc22

2007046801

ISBN 978-0-8077-4845-9 (cloth)

Printed on acid-free paper
Manufactured in the United States of America

15 14 13 12 11 10 09 08 8 7 6 5 4 3 2 1

Contents

Foreword

THERE ARE probably fewer than 10 good studies in the literature on high school reform. Supovitz and Weinbaum's book stands out, making an original and thorough contribution to school reform. Starting with a concise and critical review of the history of implementation research, the authors serve notice that their study is going to be interesting, and well informed. Their sample is small enough (15 high schools), but with enough range to make it rich in possibilities, encompassing comprehensive school reform models, literacy reform, and data reform—an organizational instructional strategy, along with a curriculum strategy and a data-based strategy.

Supovitz, Weinbaum, and their colleagues then dissect the reform stories, using a creative range of analytical tools. They have a chapter on variation in implementation within and across the three models. They then show how design factors make a huge difference in terms of how the initiatives vary in emphasis or focus, in degree of complexity, in how engaging they are, and in the degree of implementation support.

An excellent chapter follows on "going with the flow" of communication. It is a tribute to the authors; throughout the book, and in this chapter in particular, they are great on drilling down to detail, but the reader never feels bogged down. The same is true of the next chapter, which examines the complex topic of resistance to reform. Another chapter furnishes great insights on the central office. A simple but powerful framework is used to examine the degree of coupling, capacity, and alignment between schools and districts; we see the consequences of mismatches between schools and their districts across the three dimensions, and we see what happens when there is congruence between the two levels. The book culminates with a strong finish, returning us to the study of implementation, but advancing the field considerably through the discussion of "refracted reform" and how it dynamically unfolds in specific situations under different conditions.

This is a well-written, interesting, and insightful book. It ends up indirectly telling us that focusing on innovations is not the most fruitful way of improving high schools. Rather, we need to tackle the culture of high schools. Even in the selected "innovative" high schools studied, it was typical for more than a third of the teachers to operate in isolation without sharing or receiving ideas to improve teaching. If we want to change high schools, we need to focus on de-privatizing teaching, fostering learning communities among teachers, linking the work to what students are learning, and creating alternatives and choices that are more engaging for adolescents. Accomplishing this will require stronger leadership from principals and teacher leaders, closer partnership with their districts, and more external networking with other schools and agencies. In the meantime, Supovitz and Weinbaum have given us a vivid and nuanced picture of high schools when they go about taking on innovations—a great contribution to the understanding and realities of high schools today.

—Michael Fullan
Professor Emeritus, University of Toronto

Acknowledgments

THE RESEARCH in this volume was made possible by the contributions of hundreds of people across the United States. The editors and contributors are most indebted to the teachers and administrators at the 15 high schools and school districts represented in this study. To paraphrase Tennessee Williams, we have depended on the kindness of strangers. And we have been amply rewarded. These busy people took time from their work lives to welcome us into their schools and districts and to share their knowledge and experiences with us. We visited them repeatedly, peppered them with questions, surveyed them, observed them, and asked more questions. Through it all, they maintained good humor and interest in our work. In addition, we are thankful to the five external school reform organizations that agreed to participate in this study. They helped us to identify research sites, provided a wealth of information about their programs, and were more than willing to answer questions along the way. We could not have done this work without their participation. We are so very thankful to the school, district, and reform organization staff and hope that this volume can repay, even in a small way, the generosity that they showed us.

Nor would this research have been possible without financial support from the United States Department of Education's Institute of Education Sciences (Grant Number R308A96003). The grant support provided to the Consortium for Policy Research in Education (CPRE) has made possible this and other important investigations of education improvement efforts. However, the opinions expressed in this publication are those of the authors and do not necessarily reflect the views of any of the organizations named above.

We also want to thank several individuals who made particular contributions to this work. Gary Sykes and Margaret Goertz reviewed the work in this volume and offered thoughtful commentary. This work is better for their suggestions. Kelly Stanton Fair, Yolanda Green, and Connie Langland were patient and kind and careful in their preparation of this document for final publication. Working under challenging time constraints, their talents and good humor were much appreciated. Susan Fuhrman, Chair of the Management Committee at CPRE, was a driving force behind this research from the project's inception six years ago and continues to inspire us to produce and disseminate high-quality educational research. All of the staff members at CPRE have been extremely supportive of this work over the past several years. Marianna Wakulowska and Debi Slatkin deserve particular mention for their help in keeping what came to be known as "Project 3" on budget and running smoothly for many years.

We are also grateful to the staff at Teachers College Press. We are particularly indebted to Brian Ellerbeck for his enthusiasm for our project and his leadership in bringing it to the public. We also thank Susan Liddicoat, Lyn Grossman, Tamar Elster, Nancy Power, and Adee Braun for the role that they played in bringing this volume to fruition.

On a more personal note, we would like to thank each of the contributors represented among these chapters. It is rare to have the opportunity to search, explore, create, and write over such extended periods of time and in such good company. They all made contributions far in excess of those signified by the author credits. Working closely with them over the years has been both an honor and a privilege. Finally, we worked on this volume in a collaborative partnership and are listed alphabetically, indicating unique and complementary contributions to this work.

—The Editors

CHAPTER 1

Reform Implementation Revisited

Jonathan A. Supovitz and Elliot H. Weinbaum

IN THE POLICY environment of the first decade of the 21st century, the stakes are enormous for developing and implementing reliable educational reforms. The American education system, the cornerstone of our nation's ability to compete in the global economy, is widely seen as troubled and uneven at best. In an effort to ratchet up improvement, schools are being held accountable for the performance of their students as never before. The federal government has invested hundreds of millions of dollars in instructional interventions that can be replicated reliably and spread across the system. To that end, the U.S. Department of Education, National Science Foundation, and National Institutes of Health increasingly are sponsoring efficacy trials to develop replicable interventions. The goal is to populate a "What Works Clearinghouse" with replicable and reliable programs that schools and districts can use to spur widespread improvements. In such an environment, understanding implementation is more crucial than ever before.

Improving teaching and learning through the introduction and spread of potentially powerful external reform ideas is a strategy that educators have been trying to apply for the past century (Cremin, 1988; Cuban, 1984). Often, however, reforms don't turn out as planned, or they fail to transfer successfully from one site to another. In fact, educators have long noted how difficult it is to spread reform ideas consistently and reliably across schools or districts (Bauman, Stein, & Ireys, 1991; Berman & McLaughlin, 1976; Elmore, 1996). The pivotal question that arises from these common and disappointing experiences is whether they are due to poor program conceptualization or improper execution in the local site (Bauman, Stein, & Ireys, 1991; Boruch & Gomez, 1977; Moncher & Prinz, 1991). What exactly does happen when externally designed reforms enter into school environments, and the implementation process unfolds? How and in what ways do reforms change schools even as schools alter the intent of reforms? What motivates school faculty responses and program designer reactions? Students of educational improvement have long puzzled over why some reform ideas blossom in schools, while others wither away.

This book is a close up examination of the complex implementation process by which promising instructional reforms play out in American high schools. Until fairly recently the implementation process received much less scrutiny than its complexity merits. By its clinical definition, implementation is the fairly straightforward act of carrying out or completing a plan or order. It is simply the means for achieving a particular end or outcome. Early research on program and policy enactment was focused more on the goal itself and less on what happened along the way toward achieving that goal. Thus, researchers initially paid less attention to the implementation process than to influence on the target of a policy or program.

RESEARCH ON IMPLEMENTATION

Even 30 years ago, implementation was still considered a fairly straightforward process. Established views of policy and programmatic activity ignored or assumed implementation issues to be relatively simple (McLaughlin, 1987). Others viewed implementation as a primarily technical procedure for executing programs as planned (Carlson, 1965; Havelock, 1969). The concept of implementation "fidelity" grew out of the assumption that what is enacted should be faithful to the designer's intent. From this perspective, poor implementation often was explained as an act of willful resistance on the part of implementers for the purpose of sabotaging reforms that were inconsistent with their own agendas or power bases (Firestone, 1989; Hjern, 1982; Lipsky, 1978).

Beginning in the 1970s, as what was designed often did not match what was enacted, implementation began to receive increasing attention. During this era, Chris Argyris and Donald Schön (1974) at MIT developed the distinction between theory of action, espoused theory, and theory in use to explain the discrepancies between the theory of a program, how people understood and described the theory of a program (which often was influenced by their mental maps that reflected their understanding of the way the world worked), and the theory in use by which a program actually was enacted. Argyris and Schön's work laid some of the conceptual groundwork on which researchers began to develop theories to explain why reforms often played out differently than their designers intended.

Other researchers noted the discrepancies between program intent and enactment, and offered different perspectives. Through the groundbreaking work of Pressman and Wildavsky (1973), who described the meandering, Rube Goldberg-like process by which local government enacted federal economic development policy, we learned more about the importance, interactive nature, and variability of implementation. Implementation, Pressman and Wildavsky concluded, "may be viewed as a process of interaction between the setting of goals and actions geared towards achieving them" (p. xxi). A steady stream of research and evaluation studies conducted since then reinforced the conclusion that the impact of even the most carefully planned, best supported initiatives was unpredictable, depending on how individuals interpreted their responsibilities and acted upon them (Bardach, 1977; Cohen & Hill, 2001; Fullan, 1991; Knapp, 1997; McLaughlin, 1987; Van Meter & Van Horn, 1975).

The evolution of researchers' recognition of the nuances of implementation has been captured in several reviews of implementation research over the past 30 years. In one such review, Allan Odden (1991) gave a historical perspective of how implementation was viewed by policy researchers. Looking over federal and state policy implementation, Odden described a three-stage chronological progression of the field's understandings about implementation. In the first stage, roughly during the 1960s and 1970s, researchers focused on the conflicts between federal- and state-initiated programs and local orientations, values, and priorities. Odden interpreted this stage as implementation problems being understood largely as local resistance or inability to enact policy initiatives. In Odden's second stage, occurring approximately during the 1970s and 1980s, researchers were more sanguine as they looked beyond initial implementation toward the longer term effects of federal programs like Title I and special education services. In studying the longer term effects, researchers found enduring footprints of particular programs. These studies examined policymakers' responses to earlier findings and the tighter rules and regulations embedded in policy design. Studies in this era (Jung & Kirst, 1986; Peterson, Rabe, & Wong, 1986) found evidence that large-scale programs were being implemented.

The third stage described by Odden, occurring over the course of the 1980s, reflected the distinction between implementation and outcomes. In this stage, according to Odden, researchers began to recognize the complexity of the implementation process and started to document the trends of large implementation variability and relatively small reliable impacts. McLaughlin (1987) described this phenomenon as "implementation dominates outcomes" (p. 172). Odden's description of the evolution of implementation research provides a useful context for the attention to local micro-implementation variability that has been the focus of implementation research over the past decade.

While Odden's work emphasized the evolving understanding of policy implementation, others focused on program implementation issues. Some researchers consider policy and program implementation as distinct (Datta, 1981), because policies are framed more ambiguously and are of greater scope. Others note the similarities between the two in that both attempt to change local practice through a series of requirements and specifications.

Focusing more on programs, other researchers have investigated different facets of the implementation puzzle. Dane and Schneider (1998) examined the different factors associated with fidelity of implementation. Their review focused on contextual considerations and identified a set of factors that seemed related to fidelity of implementation:

Program adherence
Exposure to program content
Quality of program delivery
Participant engagement
Program distinctiveness

Interestingly, they found that exposure to a program was only inconsistently related to program outcomes.

In another review of the literature on program fidelity, Ruiz-Primo (2006) focused on program characteristics associated with fidelity of implementation. She identified five distinct characteristics that were related to program fidelity:

1. Program complexity had a distinct influence on fidelity; simpler programs were less likely to be changed than more complex programs.
2. Implementation time influenced fidelity, as programs with longer timelines produced more variation in enactment.
3. Programs that contained more materials and required more resources were more likely to be adjusted.
4. Training was a key consideration for improving implementation fidelity.

5. Programs with more built-in and frequent supervision were more likely to be implemented with fidelity.

Mowbray, Holter, Teague, and Bybee (2003) focused on the measurement of fidelity in their review of the implementation literature. They examined the literature with the goal of developing a set of criteria for measuring fidelity in order to derive a valid fidelity index. Thus, they were interested primarily in characteristics that could be validly measured. Their review settled on six distinct criteria:

Program length
Program intensity
Program duration
Program content
The procedures used to carry out a program
The roles and qualifications of program trainers

Even while researchers decomposed the factors associated with implementation variation, the question persists as to whether fidelity is necessary or even desirable for programs to be successful. On one hand, adjustments have the potential to violate important theoretical program design elements. On the other hand, local constraints often influence how a program can be adopted. Ridgely and Jerrell (1996) raised the question of whether variations from intended program design are weaknesses, as researchers assumed, or whether they should be considered as necessary to fit program intentions into local situations and contexts. Ruiz-Primo (2006) coined the term *degree of deviation* to assess how far an implementer can deviate from a program's design and still achieve its goals. Dusenbury, Brannigan, Falco, and Hansen (2003) considered adaptation to be "at best a double edged sword, bringing with it the possibility that the critical effective ingredients of a program may be left when the program is modified to meet the needs of the community" (p. 252).

Regardless of the conceptual debate, in the messy real world, programs and policies are highly susceptible to adjustments and adaptations throughout the implementation process. These adjustments in reality were the overriding theme of one of the most ambitious educational implementation studies ever conducted. The RAND Change Agent study described the process of 293 federally funded education projects in 18 states. In this work, RAND researchers introduced the compelling notion of *mutual adaptation* to describe the ways in which reforms were shaped by both their designers and local sites throughout the implementation process (Berman &

McLaughlin, 1978). Implementation, in the words of the RAND researchers, was "the stage where the project, as a reality, first confronts another reality—the institutional setting of the school and the district" (p. 8). According to the authors:

> Rarely are projects carried out exactly to the letter of the original design. Instead, they must be adapted into the institutional setting while the people in the schools, and the organizations those people have created, must at the same time adapt to the demands of the project. In other words, we hypothesize that innovation in schools is a process of mutual adaptation. If nothing happens to change the project, then it probably never really "met" the system. If nothing happens to change the setting, then there probably was no real implementation. (p. 8)

Since the Change Agent study, educational research in a variety of topical areas repeatedly has chronicled the uncertain nature of the implementation process. Studies of teacher professional development programs, for example, have observed how teachers tend to incorporate new knowledge into their own frames of reference, often changing the meaning of the reform in the process (Cohen & Barnes, 1993; Hill, 2001; Spillane & Zueli, 1999). As another example, research on comprehensive school reform programs regularly has documented the variability in implementation, pointing out how what is enacted is often different from the original design (Berends, Bodilly, & Kirby, 2002; Datnow, Hubbard, & Mehan, 2002; Rowan, Camburn, & Barnes, 2004; Supovitz & May, 2004). Elmore (1996) viewed these local mutations of external reform ideas as almost a pathology of the education field. He conducted a synthesis of several studies of large-scale instructional reform projects, including the progressive reform ideas of the early 1900s and the National Science Foundation curriculum reforms of the 1960s, and chronicled how these potentially powerful ideas tended to shrivel as they became widespread, replaced by more superficial and marginal rearrangements that were mere shadows of their former selves.

Evidence on the relationship between fidelity and outcomes has failed to resolve the debate about whether adaptations are desirable or harmful to achieving program ends. Gresham, Gansle, Noell, Cohen, and Rosenblum (1993) reviewed 26 behavioral intervention studies published between 1980 and 1990 that measured implementation, and found moderate and significant correlations between fidelity of implementation and outcomes. Dane and Schneider (1998) reviewed 39 drug prevention programs that had information on fidelity, and concluded that the relationship between fidelity of implementation and outcomes was inconsistent. Blakely, Mayer, Gottschalk, Schmitt, Davidson, Roitman, and Emshoff (1987) looked directly at the issue of fidelity versus adaptation in seven national education and criminal justice projects. Overall, they found that programs adopted with high fidelity were more effective than those that had been modified or adapted. They also found that localities that added to or expanded a program tended to increase its effectiveness, while local modifications to an existing program were less effective or unrelated to effectiveness. McGrew, Bond, Dietzen, and Salyers (1994) studied the implementation of a school-based mental health model and found that teachers' modifications of lessons actually were associated with improved student outcomes. Dusenbury, Brannigan, Falco, and Hansen (2003) hypothesized that this might have been due to improving the cultural sensitivity or appropriateness of the lessons for those particular students, that these actions actually improved the designed curriculum, or that only the most effective or motivated teachers made these adjustments.

In sum, despite the diversity of settings and topics, the collective body of implementation research tells a surprisingly consistent story. Variability is not the exception to the implementation experience, but the rule. Regardless of the change it may seek to bring about, any reform is likely to be buffeted by a unique mixture of local forces as it enters into, and interacts with, local context. This variability can be understood at two levels. In the conventional sense, variability can be thought of as different speeds at which the same process is accomplished. Two schools can start out implementing a program at the same time and can implement the program at different rates. But variability in implementation of a reform also can be defined as adjustments to the very program that schools are implementing. If a program fundamentally changes as it works its way through a school, then variability among schools takes on a different cast. In such cases, *what* is being implemented in one site may be subtly or fundamentally different from what is being implemented in other sites, or even within subunits of the same site. Additionally, the interpretations that reforms undergo happen at many different time points and many different levels as they work their way through the multiple layers of the education system. Thus, variability in implementation can be seen as *the* major challenge for efforts to change instructional practice systematically in American schools.

WHAT DRIVES IMPLEMENTATION VARIABILITY?

The current dominant paradigm that explains the variable process of implementation is that of individual discretion and influence. Going back to the RAND Change Agent study, the overarching explanation for local variation in implementation was the latitude of individual actors. As individuals attempted to make sense of policy, they used their beliefs, experiences, and knowledge to fashion a reaction. In reflecting on the experience of the Change Agent study, Milbrey McLaughlin (1987), one of the primary study authors, argued that "what actually is delivered . . . depends finally on the individual at the end of the line" (p. 174). This perspective, she continued, "shifts the focus of analysis away from institutions and institutional goals to individuals and individual incentives, beliefs, and capacity" (p. 174). This interpretation comported well with other emerging educational policy research, including the work on special education reform implementation by Weatherly and Lipsky (1977), who argued that policy implementation is highly dependent on individual "street-level bureaucrats."

The predominance of the individual agent as the central influence on implementation was synthesized by Spillane, Reiser, and Reimer (2002), who brought together a wide range of research to develop a cognitive framework to explain what influences the implementation process. They argued that individual sense making captured what otherwise might appear to be capricious implementation patterns. Through a detailed literature review they argued that individuals are heavily influenced by their existing cognitive structures, including their prior knowledge, beliefs, and values, which together cause them to reshape and sometimes misinterpret reform ideas. Thus, new knowledge at times is misconstrued so that it looks more like prior knowledge and produces superficial interpretations that gloss over deeper meaning. From this perspective, implementation was understood to be primarily a process of individual framing, interpreting, and constructing meaning from policy messages.

Beyond individual sense making, social interactions—by constraining, stabilizing, and providing meaning via group membership—also can have a powerful influence on how people act (Schein, 1992). The theory that social forces influence the actions of group members is based on the concept of social capital. Social capital is a "social asset by virtue of actors' connections and access to resources in the network or group of which they are members" (Lin, 2001, p. 19). According to Coleman (1988), social interactions influence people in at least four ways. First, they *establish a system of obligations and expectations* that connect people in an organization to one another. Second, the strong connections that are developed help to *define social norms* within a community. These norms define those practices that are acceptable and those that are not.

When norms of practice are in flux, or are the target of change by an outside force, the relationships between individuals in an organization can be a highly effective mode for transmitting new information. Such *trans-*

mission or diffusion of new information is the third influence of social capital identified by Coleman. The web of relationships that exist in an organization may have been created for any number of purposes—to secure a favor, pursue a political agenda, or as a result of a natural friendship affinity—but will influence people as they understand and respond to their environment. The *connection between social capital and individual sense making* is the fourth and final of Coleman's uses of social capital; in this way social capital is connected to individual human capital. Individual capability is increased, in part, through interactions with others. Through connections with others in an organization or community, individuals are able to enhance their own knowledge and skills in a particular area.

Within schools, the social relations that influence perspectives may be derived through naturally arising organic relationships between faculty members or influenced by particular embedded organizational structures. Organizational structures like departments, teams, and professional learning communities have a powerful influence on access to information and learning opportunities of group members (Coburn & Stein, 2006; Sisken, 2003; Supovitz, 2002). Such constructed communities can foster a collaborative culture within schools (DuFour & Eaker, 1998; McLaughlin & Talbert, 2001). Opportunities for shared practice can lead to "collective knowledge, shared sense-making and distributed understanding that doesn't reduce to the content of individual heads" (Brown & Duguid, 1996, p. 78). Bryk and Schneider (2002) illustrate how effective social relationships among organizational members, which they call relational trust, can play a key role in school improvement. Supovitz (2002) showed that teachers involved in teams designed explicitly to encourage communication do, in fact, demonstrate significant positive differences in the way they feel about their school involvement, collaboration, and interaction with peers.

In addition to structural characteristics, other dimensions of organizational configuration also can have a powerful influence on decision makers. Organizational theorists have long noted a set of influential forces that evolve as organizations build traditions and develop standard operating procedures. Nelson and Winter (1982) explored how organizations encode references from their history into routines that guide behavior. Daft and Weick (1984) argued that information/knowledge is stored in collective memory, based on the cumulative experiences of individuals constituting the organization. March (1991) theorized that organizations store knowledge accumulated over time from the learning of their members in the form of an organizational code that constitutes the organization's shared mental models. According to Van Maanen (1979), organizations develop a set of implicit, unwritten rules for getting along in the organization that sometimes subtly, and other times more blatantly, influence the actions of members. Schein (1978) refers to this as simply "the way we do things around here." Deal and Kennedy (1999) describe formal rituals of organizations that powerfully shape the considerations and actions of organizational members. Schools, which are some of the most entrenched institutions in our society, are heavily subject to these considerations.

In sum, the research on implementation variability helps us to understand that a complex combination of individual, social, and organizational characteristics interact and influence both the pace and content of program implementation. The research in this book builds on the knowledge base about implementation and expands our understanding of program implementation. From a variety of perspectives, the research in the following chapters illustrates ways in which individual, social, and organizational factors create interactions between programs and sites to produce the adjustments that are made as reforms are implemented in districts and schools.

CPRE STUDY OF IMPLEMENTATION VARIATION

As noted earlier, this book is a study of the implementation of complex reforms in American high schools. In it, we focus on how reforms intended to improve high school teachers' instructional practice were designed and enacted as they unfolded in particular school contexts with particular needs, capacities, and constraints. Through our studies, we focus on the variation in the implementation process and explore the reasons for that variation. Unlike other implementation studies, we did not enter into the work expecting to see high levels of fidelity, for the cavalcade of past research on reform implementation indicated that variability would be the rule rather than the exception. Instead, it was our purpose to closely examine the expected variability to understand what it looks like and why it occurred, and what distinguished cases of productive adaptation from cases of destructive mutation. Because our interest was in the variability, we decided to focus on the nexus of reform designs and schools; we looked from the top down, the bottom up, and the inside out. More formally, our research was guided by two primary research questions:

1. How do the reform ideas and practices of external change agents interact with school environments and teacher attributes to change instructional and organizational practices in high schools?
2. What factors both within and outside high schools explain differing levels of understanding and enactment of programs?

This book is an effort to shed light on these important questions about variability in implementation by looking at the introduction of external reform in a diverse sample of American high schools. It is based on a two and a half year, in-depth investigation by the Consortium for Policy Research in Education (CPRE). For the study, CPRE researchers examined the implementation of three types of external reform programs in a diverse national sample of 15 American high schools and their districts. We chose to focus on high schools for two reasons. First, high schools traditionally have received less attention than elementary schools, and there is a need for more research on the particularities of high schools. Second, our earlier research focused on high schools' response to accountability, and we sought to extend that work.

An earlier phase of this study, conducted from 2002 to 2004, focused on high school responses to different degrees of state accountability pressure. This earlier research indicated that certain responses predominated (see Gross & Goertz, 2005). These included aligning curriculum to state standards, adding basic skills or advanced academic courses, test preparation activities, additional reading programs, efforts to use data to improve instructional decision making, and organizational changes such as block scheduling or daily sustained silent reading time. The most substantive reform efforts focused on intensive reading efforts or larger school efforts of which reading was a major component. Based on these findings, we focused the second phase of our research on three types of school improvement efforts: (1) comprehensive school reforms; (2) literacy reforms; and (3) data-driven, decision-making reforms. These reform types were selected as representative of the predominant approaches to external assistance found in high schools during previous CPRE research. The three types of improvement programs are represented in this study by five particular interventions:

COMPREHENSIVE SCHOOL REFORM

1. High Schools That Work (HSTW)
2. First Things First (FTF)

LITERACY REFORM

3. Ramp-Up to Literacy (RU)
4. Penn Literacy Network (PLN)

DATA REFORM

5. SchoolNet (SN)[1]

The particular school improvement programs in each category were selected after we conducted a scan of the range of programs in each category, the strength of their designs, and evidence of their impacts. While formal evaluations of the programs were not available in most cases, we identified particular programs that had a clearly articulated vision of school and/or teacher practice. We then contacted reform providers and solicited their participation in this study. We followed the implementation process of each of these five reform programs over the course of two school years (2004–05 and 2005–06) in three high schools implementing each program. Thus, our study is based on longitudinal fieldwork in 15 high schools in 15 different districts in the United States. In order to preserve the anonymity of schools and the confidentiality of respondents, we do not use school names in this work. Instead, we identify schools using a nomenclature that conveys the reform being used and the stage of work with that reform. In this system, 1 connotes a school that had just begun its partnership with a reform organization, 2 connotes a school that was in its second year of work with a reform organization, and 3 connotes a school that had been working with the reform organization for 3 to 5 years at the start of our research. For example, FTF1 is a high school that has partnered with First Things First and was in its first year of work with that program at the time of our first data collection. This naming convention is used throughout the chapters of this volume.

The 15 schools were a diverse sample of high schools from across the nation that ranged from urban to rural, high performing to low performing, racially homogeneous to ethnically diverse. What follows is a brief synopsis of the research design, sampling strategy and resulting sample, and analysis methods for the study. For those interested, the study sample, design, and methods are described in more detail in the Appendix at the end of the book.

STUDY DESIGN AND ANALYSIS

At our request, staff from each reform provider identified three schools—two schools in their first or second year of implementation and a third "mature" site that had worked with the reform for 3 to 5 years. This sampling strategy allowed us to examine the reform at different stages in the implementation process. Early-stage schools were visited three times, mature sites once. Because our primary focus was on the process through which school staffs work with improvement programs that are new to their schools, the most experienced or mature school in our study was visited once as a point of comparison with the earlier implementing schools.

During each visit, interviews were conducted with teaching and administrative staff at the school. School staff members with both central and peripheral involvement in the reform were targeted. In addition, we interviewed staff members from the central office in each of the school districts, and staff from the reform organization. In total, our findings are based on approximately 518 semistructured interviews lasting between 30 and 60 minutes each.

In addition, in all 15 schools we administered a survey to all teaching staff in the 2004–05 academic year. The survey provided data about the enactment of components of each particular reform program, attitudes regarding the reform program, and communication among staff in each of the schools. In nine of the ten schools[2] at the earlier stages of reform implementation, we administered the survey a second time, at the end of the 2005–06 school year. Our survey findings are therefore based on 1,052 surveys from 15 schools conducted in Spring 2005 and 644 surveys from nine schools conducted in Spring 2006. The overall school response rates were quite respectable, averaging 75% and ranging between 57% and 89%.

Before and during the time of the data collection in the schools, we also collected documents and conducted interviews with staff members of the five provider organizations. Documents included promotional literature, implementation manuals, scheduling guidelines, monitoring tools, and formative and/or summative evaluations of the reforms. Overall, we conducted 20 interviews with staff members of the provider organizations. These interviews focused on the reform's goals; theories of action, learning, and schooling; and progress in the study schools.

Interviews also were conducted with central office staff members in all 15 school districts. District leaders with responsibility for selecting, supporting, or monitoring the improvement program were targeted for interviews. In total, 26 central office staff members were interviewed about the district context and the specific actions that had been taken to support reform implementation in the particular high school that was the subject of our study.

Through an iterative process in which initial exploratory data were collected and analyzed, instruments were developed and refined, and more data collected, CPRE researchers were able to investigate thematic areas that held promise in helping to understand the progress of school reform. Several etic codes were developed based on previous research into school reform efforts. These included (1) program design factors, (2) school communication patterns, (3) school leadership, and (4) district support. While these four areas are certainly not the only entry points from which to seek insight about the variability in implementation, there is plenty of past research to suggest that they are crucial factors in the implementation process. In each of these areas we sought to explain implementation and variation both among those schools working with a particular reform program as well as across the entire sample of schools. Each of the variables that served to explain, in part, the story of variability in the implementation process became a chapter in this volume.

ORGANIZATION OF THE BOOK

The remainder of this volume is organized around a series of themes that arose as we examined the experiences of the 15 high schools that were the focus of the study. Each chapter was written by a team of CPRE researchers who were part of the study design and fieldwork. Thus, while each chapter takes a different perspective on examining the data, all chapters benefit from the collaborative team process of data collection and collective analysis.

Chapter 2, written by Jennifer Mueller and Katherine Hovde, sets the stage for subsequent chapters by providing brief descriptions of what we saw unfolding in the 15 schools as they worked with the external reform programs over the course of two years. Each reform's story is told through a brief case study[3] and conveys the extent of variation that was found both within any particular improvement program as well as the types of variation evident among the five programs included in this research.

Chapters 3 through 6 analyze in detail four factors that we sought to investigate as playing a role in the reasons for variability in program implementation. Chapter 3, written by Catherine Dunn Shiffman, Matthew Riggan, Diane Massell, Matthew Goldwasser, and Joy Anderson, examines the roles played by the designs themselves in how the five reforms were adjusted and enacted in the study schools. The authors argue that the reform adjustments observed can be understood in part through an exploration of four key design factors: the emphasis placed on particular design components, the level of complexity that design components posed for teachers and administrators, strategies to engage school and district agents in enacting the reform, and the particular implementation supports (e.g., provision of technical assistance, frequency of professional development, etc.) called for in the design.

Chapter 4, written by Elliot Weinbaum, Russell Cole, Michael Weiss, and Jonathan Supovitz, examines how improvement program strategies are influenced by the communication patterns and organizational factors that exist within schools. This chapter uses social network analysis to analyze the key features of within-school communication. The authors provide strong evidence that reform programs that employ structural changes can quickly alter teacher communication around a range of professional issues. By contrast, reform programs that rely on teacher training without structural modifications have a less broad impact on teacher communication during the first few years of a reform. As a result, both traditional forms of school communication and new strategies introduced by reformers have implications for the variability in program implementation.

Chapter 5, written by Matthew Riggan and Jonathan Supovitz, explores how leadership is arrayed in the enactment of the five reform efforts in the 15 high schools. The authors argue that a full representation of leadership's influence on the implementation of reforms includes three groups: *traditional-formal leaders* (administrative leadership positions within schools), *provider-formal leaders* (leadership positions created by the reform designs themselves), and *informal leaders* (individuals who held no formal position but were identified as influential by their colleagues). The chapter analyzes the role that each type of leader plays in supporting reform. The findings suggest that distributed leadership is best understood as an organizational condition of schools rather than an intervention to be undertaken by school leaders. Interventions, including those being studied here, that are focused on the latter may overlook, or even undermine, existing leadership arrays.

Chapter 6, written by Elliot Weinbaum, Catherine Dunn Shiffman, and Margaret Goertz, investigates the role played by the district central office in supporting the efforts of the reform program. In this analysis, it becomes clear that the central office plays an influential role in helping to explain variability in reform program implementation. The authors find that central office support of the reform effort that met the expectations of the external provider consistently yielded high levels of use at the high school level. In contrast, where there was little or no central office support for a reform, we found a great deal of variation at the school level. Without active central office support, program implementation was much more dependent on factors at the school level, which are described and analyzed in other chapters of this volume.

In Chapter 7, by Jonathan Supovitz, closes with a synthesis of the findings across the chapters. We introduce a theoretical framework that emerges from both the literature on implementation and the findings from our data that explain implementation variability. Using this framework, which we call iterative refraction, we provide direct examples from the chapters that support the theory that we propose. This is done in an effort to provide a framework for future studies of reform use and planning by those involved directly in the process. The volume closes with a discussion of the implications of both the previous chapters and our framework for reform program designers, school and district leaders, and researchers.

We hope that you will keep one additional point in mind as you read this volume. All of the authors of the subsequent chapters stand in great admiration of the teachers, school administrators, central office staff members, and provider representatives who spend each day thinking about the ways in which they can help students across this country. As we have described and analyzed the work of others over the past several years, we have gained deep respect for, and value the work of, all of the people involved in the schools, districts, and improvement organizations that we were privileged to study. We are cognizant of the words of Theodore Roosevelt: "It is not the critic who counts; not the man who points out how the strong man stumbles, or where the doer of deeds could have done better. The credit belongs to the man who is actually in the arena." Our goal in the chapters that follow is not to undermine or criticize the tireless efforts of thoughtful and well-intentioned actors in the educational arena. Instead, we offer this work with the hope that it will prove helpful, that it in fact might make the work of the women and men in the educational arena more satisfying for everyone involved and more likely to yield desired outcomes.

NOTES

1. A second data-based intervention agreed to participate initially but then declined to continue when we embarked upon our data collection.

2. Although we had intended to administer a second survey in all ten of the early-implementing schools, natural disaster and subsequent school closure made this impossible in one case.

3. More detailed case studies for each of the reforms can be found on the CPRE website at www.cpre.org.

REFERENCES

Argyris, C., & Schön, D. A. (1974). *Theory in practice: Increasing professional effectiveness.* San Francisco: Jossey-Bass.

Bardach, E. (1977). *The implementation game: What happens after a bill becomes a law.* Cambridge, MA: MIT Press.

Bauman, L. J., Stein, R. E. K., & Ireys, H. T. (1991). Reinventing fidelity: The transfer of social technology among settings. *American Journal of Community Psychology, 19,* 619–639.

Berends, M., Bodilly, S., & Kirby, S. N. (2002). *Facing the challenges of whole-school reform: New American Schools after a decade.* Santa Monica, CA: RAND Corporation.

Berman, P., & McLaughlin, M. W. (1976). Implementation of educational innovation. *The Educational Forum, 40,* 345–370.

Berman, P., & McLaughlin, M. W. (1978). *Federal programs supporting educational change: Vol. VIII. Implementing and sustaining innovations.* Santa Monica, CA: RAND Corporation.

Blakely, C. H., Mayer, J. P., Gottschalk, R. G., Schmitt, N., Davidson, W., Roitman, D. B., & Emshoff, J. G. (1987). The fidelity–adaptation debate: Implications for the implementation of public sector social programs. *American Journal of Community Psychology, 15,* 253–268.

Boruch, R. R., & Gomez, H. (1977). Sensitivity, bias, and theory in impact evaluation. *Professional Psychology, 8,* 411–433.

Brown, J., & Duguid, P. (1996). Organizational learning and communities-of-practice: Toward a unified view of working, learning, and innovation. In M. D. Cohen & L. Sproull (Eds.), *Organizational learning* (pp. 58–82). Thousand Oaks, CA: Sage.

Bryk, A., & Schneider, B. (2002). *Trust in schools.* New York: Russell Sage Foundation.

Carlson, R. O. (1965). *Adoption of educational innovations.* London: Tavistock.

Coburn, C. E., & Stein, M. K. (2006). Communities of practice theory and the role of teacher professional community in policy implementation. In M. I. Honig (Ed.), *New directions in education policy implementation: Confronting complexity* (pp. 25–46). Albany: State University of New York Press.

Cohen, D. K., & Barnes, C. A. (1993). Conclusion: A new pedagogy for policy? In D. K. Cohen, M. W. McLaughlin, & J. E. Talbert (Eds.), *Teaching for understanding: Challenges for policy and practice* (pp. 240–276). San Francisco: Jossey-Bass.

Cohen, D. K., & Hill, H. C. (2001). *Learning policy: When state education reform works.* New Haven, CT: Yale University Press.

Coleman, J. S. (1988). Social capital in the creation of human capital. *American Journal of Sociology, 94,* S95–S120.

Cremin, L. A. (1988). *American education, the metropolitan experience, 1876–1980.* New York: Harper & Row.

Cuban, L. (1984). *How teachers taught: Constancy and change in American classrooms, 1890–1980.* New York: Longman.

Daft, R. L., & Weick, K. E. (1984). Toward a model of organizations as interpretation systems. *Academy of Management Review, 9*(2), 284–295.

Dane, A. V., & Schneider, B. H. (1998). Program integrity in primary and early secondary prevention: Are implementation effects out of control? *Clinical Psychology Review, 18,* 23–45.

Datnow, A., Hubbard, L., & Mehan, H. (2002). *Extending educational reform: From one school to many.* London: RoutledgeFalmer.

Datta, L. E. (1981). Damn the experts and full speed ahead: An examination of the study of federal programs supporting educational change, as evidence against directed development for local problem solving. *Evaluation Review, 5,* 5–32.

Deal, T. E., & Kennedy, A. A. (1999). *The new corporate cultures.* New York: Perseus Books.

DuFour, R., & Eaker, R. (1998). *Professional learning communities at work: Best practices for enhancing student achievement.* Bloomington, IN: National Educational Service.

Dusenbury, L., Brannigan, R., Falco, M., & Hansen, W. B. (2003). A review of research on fidelity of implementation: Implications for drug abuse prevention in school settings. *Health Education Research, 18*(2), 237–256.

Elmore, R. F. (1996). Getting to scale with good educational practice. *Harvard Educational Review, 66*(1), 1–26.

Firestone, W. A. (1989). Using reform: Conceptualizing district initiative. *Educational Evaluation Policy and Analysis, 11*(2), 151–164.

Fullan, M. G. (1991). *The new meaning of educational change.* New York: Teachers College Press.

Gresham, F. M., Gansle, K. A., Noell, G. H., Cohen, S., & Rosenblum, S. (1993). Treatment integrity of school-based behavioral intervention studies: 1980–1990. *School Psychology Review, 22,* 245–272.

Gross, B., & Goertz, M. E. (Eds.). (2005). *Holding high hopes: How high schools respond to state accountability policies* (CPRE Research Report No. RR-056). Philadelphia: University of Pennsylvania, Consortium for Policy Research in Education.

Havelock, R. G. (Ed.). (1969). *Planning for dissemination through dissemination and utilization of knowledge.* Ann Arbor: University of Michigan, Center for Research on Utilization of Scientific Knowledge.

Hill, H. C. (2001). Policy is not enough: Language and the interpretation of state standards. *American Educational Research Journal, 38*(2), 289–320.

Hjern, B. (1982). Implementation research: The link gone missing. *Journal of Public Policy, 2,* 301–308.

Jung, R. K., & Kirst, M. W. (1986). Beyond mutual adaptation, into the bully pulpit: Recent research on the federal role in education. *Educational Administration Quarterly, 22*(3), 80–109.

Knapp, M. (1997). Between systemic reforms and the mathematics and science classroom: The dynamics of innovation, implementation, and professional learning. *Review of Educational Research, 67*(2), 227–266.

Lin, N. (2001). *Social capital: A theory of social structure and action.* Cambridge, England: Cambridge University Press.

Lipsky, M. (1978). Standing the study of public policy implementation on its head. In W. D. Burnham & M. W. Weinberg (Eds.), *American politics and public policy* (pp. 391–402). Cambridge, MA: MIT Press.

March, J. G. (1991). Exploration and exploitation in organizational learning. *Organizational Science, 2,* 71–87.

McGrew, J. H., Bond, G. R., Dietzen, L., & Salyers, M. (1994). Measuring the fidelity of implementation of a mental health program model. *Journal of Consulting and Clinical Psychology, 62,* 670–678.

McLaughlin, M. W. (1987). Learning from experience: Lessons from policy implementation. *Educational Evaluation and Policy Analysis, 9*(2), 171–178.

McLaughlin, M. W., & Talbert, J. E. (2001). *Professional communities and the work of high school teaching.* Chicago: University of Chicago Press.

Moncher, F. J., & Prinz, R. J. (1991). Treatment fidelity in outcome studies. *Clinical Psychology Review*, 11, 247–266.

Mowbray, C., Holter, M. C., Teague, G. B., & Bybee, D. (2003). Fidelity criteria: Development, measurement, and validation. *American Journal of Evaluation, 24*(3), 315–340.

Nelson, R. R., & Winter, S. G. (1982). *An evolutionary theory of economic change.* Cambridge, MA: Harvard University Press.

Odden, A. (1991). New patterns of education policy implementation and challenges for the 1990s. In A. Odden (Ed.), *Educational policy implementation* (pp. 297–327). Albany: State University of New York Press.

Peterson, P., Rabe, B., & Wong, K. (1986, December 17). The real issue: Helping people, not places. *Christian Science Monitor*, p. 16.

Pressman, J. L., & Wildavsky, A. B. (1973). *Implementation: How great expectations in Washington are dashed in Oakland.* Berkeley: University of California Press.

Ridgely, M. S., & Jerrell, J. M. (1996). Analysis of three interventions for substance abuse treatment of severely mentally ill people. *Community Mental Health Journal, 32*, 561–572.

Rowan, B., Camburn, E., & Barnes, C. (2004). Benefiting from comprehensive school reform: A review of research on CSR implementation. In C. Cross (Ed.), *Putting the pieces together: Lessons from comprehensive school reform research* (pp. 1–52). Washington, DC: National Clearinghouse for Comprehensive School Reform.

Ruiz-Primo, M. A. (2006). *A multi-method and multi-source approach for studying fidelity of implementation* (CSE Report 677). Los Angeles, CA: National Center for Research on Evaluation, Standards, and Student Testing (CRESST).

Schein, E. H. (1978). *Career dynamics: Matching individual and organizational needs.* Reading, MA: Addison-Wesley.

Schein, E. H. (1992). *Organizational culture and leadership* (2nd ed.). San Francisco: Jossey-Bass.

Sisken, L. S. (2003). When an irresistible force meets an immovable object: Core lessons about high schools and accountability. In M. Carnoy, R. Elmore, & L. S. Siskin (Eds.), *The new accountability: High schools and high-stakes testing* (pp. 175–194). New York: RoutledgeFalmer.

Spillane, J. P., Reiser, B. J., & Reimer, T. (2002). Policy implementation and cognition: Reframing and refocusing implementation research. *Review of Educational Research, 72*(3), 387–431.

Spillane, J. P., & Zueli, J. S. (1999). Reform and teaching: Exploring patterns of practice in the context of national and state mathematics reforms. *Educational Evaluation and Policy Analysis, 21*(1), 1–28.

Supovitz, J. A. (2002). Developing communities of practice. *Teachers College Record, 104*(8), 1591–1626.

Supovitz, J. A., & May, H. (2004). A study of the links between implementation and effectiveness of the America's Choice comprehensive school reform design. *Journal of Education for Students Placed at Risk, 9*(4), 389–419.

Van Maanen, J. (1979). The fact of fiction in organizational ethnography. *Administrative Science Quarterly, 24*(4), 539–550.

Van Meter, D. S., & Van Horn, C. E. (1975). The policy implementation process: A conceptual framework. *Administration and Society, 6*(4), 445–486.

Weatherly, R., & Lipsky, M. (1977). Street-level bureaucrats and institutional innovation: Implementing special-education reform. *Harvard Educational Review, 47*(2), 171–197.

CHAPTER 2

Theme and Variation in the Enactment of Reform: Case Studies

Jennifer A. Mueller and Katherine H. Hovde

THIS CHAPTER describes the variation in implementation that we observed among the 15 high schools included in this study. The chapter is organized into case studies of the five external reforms we examined.[1] Each case study briefly outlines the reform's goals and the primary strategies for attaining them. We then describe the manner in which the reform was enacted in three schools, and teachers' and administrators' perceptions of the reform's effects. The purpose of these five brief case studies is twofold. First, they provide the reader with a basic understanding of the rationale and intent of each reform as a foundation for the subsequent chapters in this book. Second, they highlight the variation we observed in reform enactment within as well as across the reforms. A concluding section discusses the types of variations observed.

As noted in Chapter 1, variation in implementation is the norm rather than the exception in school reform. Such variation was widely evident among the high schools in this study. Within each reform, schools fashioned different interpretations of how the reform should be enacted, emphasized different aspects or components of the reform, and progressed at different rates in enacting their version of the reform. Indeed, our analysis suggests that there was as much variation in reform implementation *within* the reforms as there was *across* them.

We found that schools and districts both consciously and unconsciously adapted reforms to fit the context into which they were introduced. Even given the fact that schools and districts were adapting reforms, they made different amounts of progress in implementing the "version" of the reform program that they had built. This variation, in turn, affected the extent to which teachers changed their classroom practices in ways envisioned by the reform program designers. Examples and further elaboration of each of these types of variations can be found in the case studies that compose the bulk of this chapter.

There are a number of important caveats or limitations to the data presented in this chapter. First, although our analysis drew from survey data and interviews at the school, district, and school reform provider organizations, the case studies are weighted toward school-level interview data. Second, given the short time the majority of our schools had been working with the various reforms, our discussion of effects is both preliminary and based almost exclusively on the perceptions and/or expectations of school-level actors. The reason for their inclusion here is not to ascertain whether the reform "worked" or was implemented appropriately, but rather to capture cross-school variation in teacher and administrator perceptions of reform effects.

Finally, it is important to note that the case studies that follow are not intended as summative evaluations of either the external school reforms or the high schools. As described in Chapter 1, this study was not designed to assess outcomes, nor did we construct measures of implementation as previous analyses of school reform have attempted (Berends, Kirby, Naftel, & McKelvey, 2001). Instead, we focused on the distinct ways in which reforms were constructed and enacted in each school, and the factors that influenced that process. Where we discuss implementation progress or effects, our analysis is based on survey and interview data of teachers' perceptions of reform enactment and its consequences.

HIGH SCHOOLS THAT WORK

Overview

High Schools That Work (HSTW) aims to improve student achievement by creating "a culture of high expectations and continuous improvement in high schools" (Southern Regional Education Board [SREB], 2005, p. 2). The reform calls for high academic standards, rigorous curriculum, and increased graduation requirements. Teachers are expected to adopt instructional and assessment practices that hold all students to the same high standards, and to provide students with extra help and opportunities to revise their work until those standards are met. Student engagement is central to the reform's instructional approach. HSTW is based on the premise that for students to be engaged, they must develop strong relationships with teachers and see the purpose and relevance of their academic learning beyond high school. To those ends, the reform calls for the creation of an advisory system and closer linkages between academic and career studies. These principles are embodied in 10 "key practices" that are at the heart of the HSTW design:

1. High expectations
2. Program of study
3. Academic studies
4. Career/technical studies
5. Work-based learning
6. Teachers working together
7. Students actively engaged
8. Guidance
9. Extra help
10. Culture of continuous improvement (SREB, 2005)

Support for each of these practices is provided in the form of professional development (both on- and off-site), participation in a network of schools implementing HSTW, and on-site technical assistance from an HSTW staff member.

While schools implementing the reform are expected to adopt all of these practices, they have considerable latitude in determining the sequence, prioritization, and specific strategies for doing so. School change in the HSTW design relies on teacher engagement, empowerment, and collaboration. Once a school has entered into a contractual relationship with HSTW, it participates in a technical assistance visit (TAV) comprising internal and external evaluation. The TAV is designed to establish the basis for the school improvement plan (SIP). School staff then are organized into issue-driven groups, called focus teams. Focus teams plan, lead, and evaluate the implementation of schoolwide organizational and instructional change. The goal is to build consensus around the need to change, then to empower teachers to enact changes deemed necessary. Through ongoing teacher collaboration and reflection, a culture of continuous improvement emerges.

Once the reform agenda has been established, the focus teams begin the work of implementing reform components aligned with key practices. For example, increasing graduation requirements is a clear strategy for raising expectations. Establishing student advisory systems, family outreach programs, or small learning communities supports the goals of improving student engagement, providing guidance, and offering extra support where needed. Depending on the specific component or practice a school decides to adopt, HSTW connects it with aligned professional development opportunities, including attendance at conferences, site visits to schools that have successfully adopted HSTW practices, or direct training by HSTW or affiliated staff. Provider staff members support implementation at the school level, working closely with principals and other leaders of the reform effort, responding to the information and resource needs of school staff, and disseminating information about resources and professional development opportunities available to schools. Schools monitor their progress in implementation through feedback from provider staff members and teachers, both informally and through annual surveys. In addition, schools are expected to review student performance data to identify challenges and to implement new programs or practices as needed.

Like most reforms, HSTW has evolved over time. As a result, different cohorts of schools have experienced different types of support. For example, over the past two years the provider has focused on building leadership capacity, particularly at the school level. These efforts have focused on both the role of principals and the importance of shared decision making. Among the schools in this study, however, participation in leadership professional development was limited.

Enactment

Engagement and participation in HSTW at the three schools depended on how the reform agenda for each school was formulated. Teachers, while in some cases empowered to enact the reform agenda, had little involvement in its formulation. At all three schools, the initial decision to partner with HSTW was made by a small minority of school staff, if not by the principal alone. It appeared that while many teachers were not well informed about the reform prior to adoption, overall awareness increased rapidly thereafter.

The primary vehicle for engaging teachers was focus teams, and across the three schools participation was widespread. There was, however, considerable variation in the depth of enactment within and across schools. It appeared that the inconsistency in focus team function (and thus teacher engagement) was related to school-level, roll-out strategy. At the two early-implementing schools (HSTW1 and HSTW2),[2] in particular, it seemed that the agenda for reform was determined prior to the formation of the teams, rather than being shaped by the focus teams themselves. Focus teams whose work centered on high-priority agenda items thrived, while others were marginalized. What is clear is that the roll-out process in these two schools varied from the intent of the reform. Rather than engendering teacher buy-in through the establishment of a reform agenda, the teams were a product of a reform agenda that had already been established. High-priority agenda items (components of the reform) that were emphasized and supported by leadership were most likely to be fully implemented.

At all three schools, progress was reported on four major HSTW components. First, staff at the three schools reported taking steps toward increasing rigor of the curriculum. Using common syllabi was a popular way to do this, more common than end-of-course exams. Second, all three schools implemented an advisory program, although the frequency with which the advisory groups met and the quality of the advisory programs varied across the three schools.

Third, ninth-grade academies were focal points of implementation at two schools. The ninth-grade academy was the centerpiece of the reform at HSTW2, and was viewed as a critical aspect of the reform at that school. At HSTW1, the creation of the ninth-grade academy coincided with the school's application for a small learning community grant. Teachers generally seemed to understand the purpose for creating the academy, but voiced concern that it was too much change too quickly, given all of the other reform components being implemented. Finally, teachers at all three schools reported that connections between academic and vocational classes were being made in their classrooms. This was done most frequently at HSTW3, which had the most substantial vocational program, and where teachers reported feeling the best prepared to make such connections. At the other two schools, teachers reported linking academics and vocational classes, but there was less assurance about how prepared they felt to do so.

Perceived Effects

In general, teachers understood the basic tenets of HSTW and accepted that increasing expectations for all students was a worthy goal. However, teachers interpreted the HSTW philosophy differently and varied in the degree to which they embraced that philosophy. At HSTW1 and HSTW2, teachers who worked on high-priority components of the reform were more likely to value it than those whose work was more marginal. At HSTW3, teachers who were involved with HSTW seemed to have an overall positive perception of the reform and felt that its goals were good and realistic. And although teachers at all three schools increasingly understood that HSTW required a transition to a highly rigorous curriculum, evidence of changes in practice reflecting this understanding was scant.

It appeared that most teachers selectively added to their repertoire specific practices that they found useful or effective with their students. All three schools took steps to make the curriculum and/or graduation requirements more rigorous. Some teachers suggested that their teaching reflected this increase in rigor; in most cases, however, teachers struggled to define this change or to offer examples from their own practice. It appeared that while increases in requirements or changes in curriculum were concrete and easily identified, increasing the rigor of instruction was far more abstract and therefore difficult to realize. In contrast, a small group of teachers at two of the schools, who were heavily involved in implementing the reform, credited HSTW with effecting deep change in the way they worked. At HSTW2, for example, a small number of teachers described the reform as transformative, citing professional collaboration and teacher responsibility for student success as new norms of practice instilled by the reform. In sum, teachers whose work was central to the reform were highly supportive of the reform effort and most inclined to report that HSTW had influenced their practice.

Leadership played an important role in implementation of HSTW at all three schools (see Chapter 5, in this volume). There is little evidence, however, that the reform influenced the practice of those in formal leadership positions at the school level, regardless of whether their practices aligned or conflicted with its demands. There is more evidence that implementation of HSTW facilitated the emergence of new leaders. Specifically, individuals who played leadership roles on focus teams charged with implementing key components of the reform generally were viewed as leaders—either for the reform or more generally—by their peers.

The focus team structure created new communication patterns at all three schools (see Chapter 4, this volume). The teams were generally cross-disciplinary and thus represented a significant departure from the departmental structure that was in place prior to the adoption of HSTW. The relative strengths of these new communication networks varied and seemed to correspond with how effectively a focus team functioned. Teachers in high-functioning focus teams, or those who otherwise were heavily involved in the reform, tended to report improved communication and collaboration among teachers as an outcome of HSTW. It is worth noting that some teachers suggested that HSTW had undermined collaboration and communication, either by weakening familiar departmental structures or by dividing the school into pro- and anti-reform factions (although in these cases leadership was clearly a contributing factor as well).

Generally, there was agreement among school, district, and provider staff that HSTW would be sustained at all three schools. This sentiment was strongest at HSTW3, the mature school, and was somewhat less strong at the other two schools. At the two schools where the future of HSTW was less certain, resources and leadership were cited as potential factors affecting sustainability. In addition, outcomes (i.e., student test scores) influenced sustainability. Teachers noted that if student test scores improved, the case for continuing with the reform would be strengthened. Nevertheless, teachers at all three schools also suggested that HSTW had improved student behavior and attitudes toward school.

FIRST THINGS FIRST

Overview

First Things First (FTF) is a whole-school reform that endeavors to help schools do three things: (1) improve relationships among teachers, students, and parents; (2) improve instructional practices; and (3) reallocate resources to support the first two goals. Involvement with FTF begins when a school or district expresses interest in the reform. FTF calls for the buy-in and support of key leaders—the superintendent, school board, and school administrators—but does not require formal sign-off from other key stakeholders such as faculty leaders, parent groups, students, or community leaders, arguing that "buy-in does not occur for the vast majority of these stakeholders until the reform is implemented and shows early signs of success that are meaningful to them" (Connell, 2002, p. 2). FTF staff members participate in constituency-building activities before and during implementation in order to ensure that stakeholders understand their roles in the reform effort. Once buy-in from key leaders has been secured, several school and district staff members are identified as study group facilitators and a school improvement facilitator (SIF) is selected. These individuals are trained by FTF and prepare (with FTF) to introduce the reform to the entire school at the beginning of the planning year.

The FTF design relies on three main implementation strategies. First, FTF requires that all high schools establish thematically oriented small learning communities (SLCs) in which teachers and students will spend the majority of their instructional time. Teachers share common planning time with their SLC team members and will be involved in a process of ongoing professional conversation and instructional improvement. Each SLC is led by an SLC coordinator selected by the faculty. Second, schools establish a family advocacy system (FAS) in which small groups of students meet with an adult mentor (family advocate) on a regular basis. The goal of the FAS is to ensure that every student feels connected with an adult in the school and has a place to discuss personal and academic issues of concern. FAS assignments are expected to be in place by the start of the first implementation year, and each family advocate is also responsible for regular communication with parents. Third, FTF has developed a system of monitoring and professional development that seeks to improve practices around student engagement, course alignment, and the rigor of high school content and instruction. FTF also requires longer instructional periods through block scheduling.

In FTF's theory of action, the combination of strategies described above fosters seven critical features in the school. For students, there will be

1. Continuity of care
2. More and personalized instructional time
3. High, clear, fair academic and content standards
4. Enriched and diverse opportunities to learn, perform, and be recognized

For adults, there will be

5. Empowerment and expectations for all staff to improve instruction
6. More flexibility in the allocation of resources
7. Collective responsibility for student outcomes (Institute for Research and Reform in Education, n.d.)

Enactment

In all three FTF schools, we found teachers and administrators to be generally well informed about FTF, with their understanding of the reform growing over time in the early-implementing schools.[3] At the mature school (FTF3), many teachers talked knowledgeably about FTF components and goals, without necessarily associating them with FTF. This is a reflection both of the reform's assimilation into school culture and practice as well as the principal's approach to communicating about FTF. District staff members in all three districts were aware of their respective schools' implementation of FTF. The FTF1 and FTF2 districts were involved in the partnership with FTF, but their involvement was quite different. While the FTF1 district's own awareness and broader participation in FTF appeared to influence the use of specific reform elements at the school level, the state and FTF2 district placed a number of demands on the school, which diverted some of the school's attention and resources to other requirements. The FTF3 district was structured to give schools far more autonomy than in the other two districts, and the district administration, although aware of FTF's work with the school, was uninvolved.

In all of the schools, FTF worked with staff to form SLCs according to individual school preferences and needs. SLCs were meeting regularly at all three schools and were being used both to improve instructional practices and to build relationships among teachers and students. There was reported variation in the quality of the SLCs' functioning in all three schools, which often was attributed to leadership and turnover issues. FASs were also in place in all three schools, although teachers reported less consistent use and satisfaction with this component than with the SLCs. This was particularly true in the two schools that were still relatively early in their implementation of FTF. At FTF1, dissatisfaction with the FAS led to modifications, while at FTF2, the FAS appeared to be a low priority for school leaders in comparison with the effort directed at curricular and instructional issues (largely prompted by state pressure). At FTF3, in contrast, both the SLCs and the FAS were highly embedded features of the school and were cited by teachers as important elements of their ongoing efforts to improve student achievement.

With regard to instructional improvement, all three schools had instituted a block schedule, and FTF had provided training to administrators on how to measure a host of outcomes and implementation benchmarks. FTF also provided training to teachers, SIFs, and SLC coordinators on ways to increase student engagement, as well as the use of several protocols to prompt and guide conversations about instruction within SLCs. Staff understanding and use of these tools were most robust at the school that had been working with FTF for the longest period of time. The earlier implementing schools struggled with their use of the tools intended to review teacher planning and practice, and FTF1 requested additional assistance from the provider in this regard. Although there were some cross-SLC efforts to look at instructional content and standards by discipline in at least one school (FTF1), these were at a very preliminary stage.

Perceived Effects

Across all three schools, interviewees generally reported that FTF had helped build relationships in the schools (among both staff and students) and believed that these new relationships were helpful in improving student behavior and school climate. Several interviewees reported an increased sense of accountability among teachers both to one another and to students. They also reported finding peers in their SLCs to be useful professional resources. The reform also placed increased responsibility for instructional improvement on the SIF and SLC coordinators, and created new communication patterns in the school as teachers sought out and found new sources of advice and guidance about their professional practice.

Perceptions about the sustainability of the reform were shaped largely by issues of school and district leadership, as well as the larger accountability environment. Even at FTF3, where the reform was most entrenched and enjoyed widespread support, interviewees were unsure whether FTF would continue if the very supportive principal were to leave. At FTF2, district turmoil and a history of policy and reform churn cast doubt on the overall sustainability of FTF at the school. At FTF1, a multiyear contract with FTF, combined with a supportive principal and wider district involvement, convinced most staff that FTF would get at least a multiyear trial in the school. We also found that teachers' initial work and success with the reform played a significant role in predicting their ongoing commitment to the reform and the predictions they made about its sustainability. Staff with distinct roles in the reform effort (e.g., SLC coordinators) were generally the most committed to seeing FTF continue.

Teachers were split about whether the changes advocated by FTF would result in improved student achievement. Between 41% and 65% of teachers across the three schools agreed with the statement: "The changes called for by FTF are helping, or will help, my students to reach higher levels of achievement." In general, staff at FTF1 and FTF2 felt it was too early in the implementation of the reform to see any widespread changes in student behavior or achievement. Only at FTF3 did interviewees credit FTF with fostering a school climate that, at a minimum, created a safe haven for students and encouraged them to come to school.

RAMP-UP TO LITERACY

Overview

The goal of Ramp-Up to Literacy (RU) is to bring students who are reading 1 to 2 years below grade level up to grade level and, after 1 or 2 years, prepare them for regular English courses. To accomplish this task, the provider, the National Center for Education and the Economy (NCEE), developed two English courses (RUI and RUII) with their own curriculum and approach to instruction. These courses are intended to be taught by selected teachers to a specific group of students; RU is not designed as a whole-school reform. Selected teachers are provided with a series of formal professional development opportunities, and the RU courses include curriculum and supporting materials. The focus of the professional development is on changing teachers' understanding of, and strategies for addressing, poor reading. Schools are required to purchase classroom libraries with books categorized by reading ability for every RU classroom, and teachers must use these texts to guide students in their independent reading. RU students also are required to spend time reading to and tutoring elementary students (cross-age tutoring). Additionally, the reform calls for a number of organizational changes, particularly in scheduling. RU requires 90-minute time blocks and a maximum class size of 20 students. Students are evaluated before being placed in RUI (targeting) and then evaluated again after their first year. If necessary, they are to continue in RU for a second year (RUII) with the same teacher (looping). Involvement of instructional coaches and others in supervisory positions in RU training is not required by the reform, but is recommended by NCEE. The cost of including supervisory staff in such training, however, is not included in the basic costs of the reform.

RU's theory of student learning assumes that optimal learning conditions occur when the student tackles material that is new enough to be interesting and challenging, but not so difficult as to be frustrating. The RU model of instruction consists of a sequence of steps in which teachers first model a task, then perform the task with student assistance. Next, students perform the task while the teacher helps. Finally, the student performs the task as the teacher observes. The reform follows a workshop model of instruction built around a prescribed set of routines and rituals, and identifies how much time should be spent on the various routines. The written curriculum and materials also cue teachers with regard to when and how to use tools, techniques, and routines.

RU initially was included as part of NCEE's comprehensive school reform package, America's Choice (AC), and has evolved over time. Although the overall philosophy and many elements of RU have remained the same, implementation experience has prompted NCEE to make alterations. None of the schools implementing RU in this study were using the most current version of RU, which, among other changes, incorporates more writing than earlier versions.

Enactment

All three RU schools struggled with low student achievement and poor performance on state tests, and all served majority low-income populations. The districts played a part in introducing RU to all three schools, although the role of each district differed considerably in other respects. Finally, in all three schools, our results were complicated by the presence of other reforms. Two of the schools (RU1 and RU3) were implementing the full AC reform, while the third school (RU2) introduced some aspects of another reform in the final year of the study.[4]

All three schools had trained RU teachers and were implementing the reform, but the size and character of RU varied considerably across the three schools. At RU1, approximately one third of incoming ninth graders were placed in RU; at RU2, about half were placed in RU; and at RU3, virtually all incoming ninth graders were placed in RU. There were two RU teachers at RU1,[5] seven at RU2 the first year of the study and five the second, and five at RU3. The majority of teachers teaching RU classes had direct training by NCEE, although by the last year of the study, the RU2 district had taken over training of RU teachers.

All three districts provided some (if not always sufficient) financial support for RU, but only the RU2 and RU3 districts provided instructional support. Both these districts were supporting other schools implementing RU in addition to the schools included in the study. Both RU1 and RU3 received some support directly from NCEE (through the AC contract), although the support was perceived as diminishing over time. All three schools had a strong school-level advocate(s) for RU, as well as instructional support for RU teachers through literacy and/or instructional coaches. Teachers at RU2 and RU3 also mentioned relying on considerable collegial support.

Despite the fact that RU is designed as a reform targeted to selected teachers, we saw some spread of RU ideas at all three schools, although here too there was wide variation. For example, at RU2, ninth-grade content teachers changed their lesson structure, materials, and vocabulary to mirror concepts and techniques being used in RU classes. This use of RU as a schoolwide instructional model was particularly notable at RU2, given that the school was not also implementing AC.

Additional adaptations to and departures from RU occurred at the district, school, and individual teacher levels. For example, the RU2 district negotiated changes to the RU curriculum with NCEE, including switching literature selections and incorporating state writing requirements. Neither RU1 nor RU3 was implementing the targeting, looping, and graduation aspects of the reform—RU1 offered only one rather than two years of RU, while RU3 sent all ninth-grade RU students into a second year of RU, as opposed to graduating out those who had attained grade level. All three schools had difficulty targeting students who were only one or two years below grade level. While RU2, with the help of the district, had overcome this challenge by the final year of this study, teachers at the other two schools said they had students in the class who were more than two years below grade level. RU3 also was unable to maintain the full 90-minute block for RU. RU1 never implemented cross-site tutoring, while RU3 had abandoned this component prior to the start of this study.

In addition to structural departures from the RU design, we also found considerable variation in the frequency with which RU teachers reported using RU techniques. Much of this variation appeared to be individual, rather than related to school factors. Teachers reported more frequently using strategies that required little change to their instruction (e.g., independent reading, guided reading) than strategies that further diverged from their current practice (e.g., conducting reading conferences with small groups of students). For example, all RU teachers reported having their students do independent reading every day, whereas most held reading conferences much less frequently or not at all.

Perceived Effects

RU teachers across the three schools mostly understood the goals of the reform in a manner consistent with the NCEE literature. In addition, school instructional coaches and lead teachers generally had a strong and nuanced understanding of the reform. Not surprisingly, in the districts more closely involved with the reform (RU2 and RU3), understanding of the reform as conveyed by district staff was also much greater than at RU1, where the district had only a peripheral role. Most non-RU teachers received their information secondhand (from administrators or other teachers), and their understanding of reform goals and specifics varied. At RU1, where RU was a targeted program, schoolwide knowledge and understanding of the reform were lowest, although they improved over time. Knowledge of RU was much higher at RU3 and highest at RU2. While our study cannot establish causal links, it is worth noting that both the district and the school administration at RU2 made a deliberate effort to educate staff about RU and the issue of literacy.

Almost all RU teachers reported a positive impact of the reform on instructional practices and a strong effect on student and teacher motivation. These effects were attributed to NCEE-led trainings, as well as to seeing positive results of the reform in the classroom. Almost all teachers, administrators, and district staff interviewed saw RU as valuable and as improving student engagement and motivation to read. Teachers differed, however, as to whether they believed that the reform was capable of improving skills sufficiently within the recommended time period to enable students to reach grade level and, as importantly, to improve test scores. As noted previously, even among RU teachers, there was variation in the reported frequency with which teachers used various RU techniques. Although all RU teachers interviewed believed they were "doing the program," reports from coaches, supervisors, and NCEE staff members indicated that some teachers were better able to adhere to RU than others. Some, for example, omitted or infrequently used groupwork, and others inserted their own curricular preferences in place of, or in addition to, the prescribed course selections.

Interviewees at RU1 and RU3 expressed some doubts as to the sustainability of RU at their schools. We also found a disconnect between the perceived sustainability of RU at the individual and school levels at these schools. Many RU teachers talked about continuing to "teach RU" or use elements of the reform regardless of its formal continuation at their school. Perceived threats to the reform's sustainability at the school level included leadership and teacher turnover (RU1), lack of resources (RU1 and RU3), the pursuit of new funding sources (RU3), and accountability pressures (RU1 and RU3). At RU2, interviewees uniformly viewed the program as successful, and foresaw no potential threats to sustainability. Continued district support and an increase in test scores helped to bolster this perception, despite the fact that RU student scores had not been disaggregated and any attribution of the increase to the presence of RU was probably premature.

PENN LITERACY NETWORK

Overview

The Penn Literacy Network (PLN) is primarily a professional development model focused on training individual teachers in literacy strategies. PLN does not focus on changing a school's organizational structure or directly changing school culture outside the classroom. Instead, it targets individual teachers who are interested in improving their knowledge and skills around literacy instruction. By increasing the capacity of teachers to engage in literacy instruction, PLN seeks to have a transformative effect on instruction and student achievement not only in reading and language arts, but in all subjects.

PLN is run by a small staff that provides on-site training through staff development workshops, graduate-level coursework, and mentoring programs on a fee-for-service basis. PLN courses are credit-bearing, graduate-level, continuing education courses that are taught on-site. Each course is approximately 30 hours and typically meets every other week. Currently, more than 10 courses are available. Workshops are often "mini" versions of the courses and are available as a multiday workshop series or a single or half-day session. Workshops usually are conducted during in-school professional development time. A mentor is a PLN staff person (a facilitator) who works with teachers throughout the school year to implement PLN strategies. Mentoring occurs in conjunction with PLN courses and workshops. The focus is on providing in-school support through observation, discussion, and feedback. PLN staff believe their work becomes more effective when schools can add the mentoring component to the package of services purchased.

Typically, PLN is introduced into a school or district through a personal relationship with a district administrator, school leader, or teacher who has had prior experience with or training from PLN. When PLN is offered at a school, PLN staff members seek a working relationship with a district leader. Who takes on this role is left up to the district, and the exact role and responsibilities of this person are not specified by PLN. PLN courses and workshops enroll cohorts of teachers of similar grade levels (e.g., elementary or secondary), and courses usually meet every other week throughout the school year. PLN's introductory course (Course 1) is considered the fundamental course and is the first one offered at schools that partner with PLN. Participation in PLN professional development is optional because PLN believes that voluntary participation enhances teacher buy-in and commitment. Initial interest in the first PLN course to be offered at a school is built through an introductory presentation to all faculty. Continued and expanded interest is to stem from teachers who have taken a PLN course sharing their experiences with others. Ultimately, PLN hopes all teachers in a school will take courses and use its strategies. To accomplish this, PLN depends on a word-of-mouth strategy for spread not only across teachers within a school but also from school to school, and district to district.

More recently, in response to the changing accountability environment in which schools operate, PLN has worked with a few schools to adapt its design so it can be implemented as a schoolwide model.[6] In this form, the PLN design depends on the needs of the school requesting the adaptation. It is important to note that even as a schoolwide reform, PLN is still very much focused on the individual teacher and classroom, and training teachers in literacy strategies is still at the heart of the design.

Enactment

All three central offices played a critical role in the introduction of PLN to the schools in this study. At PLN1 and PLN2, the reform was brought in as a district-wide (K–12) initiative, spearheaded by an individual or group of individuals at the district level. PLN1 and PLN2 were located in suburban districts, and each school was the only high school in its district. Both districts had above-average student performance and met, or just nearly missed meeting, state and federal performance targets in recent years. At PLN3, two teachers initially introduced PLN in its traditional form. However, as a school in a poor and low-performing district, PLN3 was granted additional financial assistance from the state. In order to receive the additional state aid, the district worked with state and PLN staff to use PLN as a whole-school reform. But when PLN was taken schoolwide, the effort was advanced largely by the district, in particular the district superintendent. In contrast, PLN1 and PLN2 were implementing the traditional form of PLN. At the school level, general awareness of PLN was widespread at all three schools. Nearly all teachers were introduced to PLN through presentations led by a PLN facilitator, which served as a way to inform teachers about PLN and the opportunity to sign up for Course 1.

At the schools in this study, the scale of participation reflected the form of PLN being implemented—traditional or schoolwide. At the two early-implementing schools, where PLN was in its traditional form, it was enacted in accordance with its design in the first year: Course 1 was offered at both schools. Participation was very limited; seven teachers at each school enrolled in the PLN course. At PLN1 the seven participating teachers represent 11% of the faculty, and at PLN2 seven represent 14%. The following year, however, enactment differed at the two schools. PLN1 dropped the reform at the high school, and at PLN2 the only option was to enroll in a district-wide (K–12) PLN course. Low interest and participation rates were cited as the reasons for the changes that occurred at both schools from year 1 to year 2 of the study.

Enactment at PLN3 looked quite different than it did at the other two schools. In order to comply with a whole-school reform state mandate, modifications to PLN's traditional design were made so all teachers would receive some level of training. PLN-led, in-school professional development workshops, PLN courses, and teacher-led PLN sessions were made available. Over time, five different PLN courses were offered at the school, and about one half of the teachers enrolled in at least one course. PLN3 also monitored classroom-level use of PLN. For example, teachers were required to list PLN strategies on their lesson plans, and PLN strategies were included on teacher observation checklists used by administrators.

The two schools that chose to sign up for the PLN mentoring add-on had quite different experiences. Teachers at PLN2 were visited only two times and were not satisfied with the support received from their mentor, whereas teachers at PLN3 were visited more frequently and were generally pleased with their mentor. Ultimately, both schools decided not to renew the mentoring option in the second year of the study, at PLN2 because teachers were mostly dissatisfied and at PLN3 because the school received less state aid than expected.

Perceived Effects

Participating teachers[7] had a relatively clear understanding that PLN focused on training teachers in literacy strategies for use in all content areas. Across the three schools, participating teachers perceived PLN to be valuable, stating that it was a "good fit" for their school.

The scale of change at the three PLN schools in this study reflected the form of PLN at each school (traditional or schoolwide). Only the subset of teachers who enrolled in a course at the two traditional-design schools described changes in behavior and instructional practice, whereas most, if not all, teachers at the third school reported changes in behavior and instructional practice as a result of PLN. Survey data show that participating teachers across the three schools felt confident with regard to their ability to use PLN strategies. However, teachers were split roughly down the middle about whether PLN required them to make major changes in their instructional practice. Teachers tended to incorporate PLN strategies that aligned with their existing practice, while downplaying strategies that significantly challenged or altered it. The further a strategy required teachers to depart from their typical classroom practice, the less likely they were to report using that strategy with regularity, irrespective of their sense of preparedness and capability. Looking more specifically at PLN3, where all teachers were to use PLN, the extent to which teachers reportedly changed their instructional practice also appeared to be associated with the type of PLN training a teacher underwent. Different levels of exposure to PLN (workshops versus courses) seemed to have an impact on teacher understanding and use of the program.

Teachers credited PLN with having positive effects on students. At the classroom level, teachers at all three schools believed students were more engaged and motivated in class and were reading, writing, and speaking better as a result of PLN strategies. At PLN3, teachers and administrators also credited schoolwide changes in student performance (e.g., increases in state test scores) to PLN.

PLN's emphasis on voluntary teacher participation and word-of-mouth dissemination strategy has strong implications for sustainability, as was evident at each of the three schools. PLN was discontinued at PLN1 in the second year of this study. And while a second course was offered at PLN2 in the second year, teachers suspected, and district staff confirmed, that the sustainability of PLN at the school was at risk. At both schools, garnering enough teachers to enroll in PLN courses at the school was a significant challenge. At PLN3, where implementation was schoolwide, teachers generally attributed the "sticking power" of PLN to the fact that it was not very intrusive. In addition, the principal commented that PLN was pretty much entrenched, and saw no reason to change it. Sustainability of PLN, however, was also dependent on external factors. Some interviewees predicted that shortfalls in state aid, coupled with the potential for other mandated initiatives to distract the school from current reform efforts through PLN, might impact the future sustainability of the reform at PLN3.

We also noted a discrepancy in perceptions of sustainability at the individual and institutional levels. Even though the sustainability of PLN was at least somewhat in question at each school (much more so at PLN1 and PLN2 than at PLN3), teachers at all three schools said they would continue to use PLN strategies in their classrooms whether or not PLN was formally continued at their school. Teachers at each school attributed this decision to the fact that they highly valued the strategies learned from PLN and saw positive impact on the students in their classrooms.

SCHOOLNET

Overview

SchoolNet (SN) is designed to help district and school staff use data to increase academic achievement. The reform postulates that through data-driven, decision-making practices (e.g., analyzing data, organizing curriculum, tracking instruction, measuring performance, and reporting results), teachers and administrators will gain increased familiarity with their students' strengths and needs and will tailor their responses to lead to higher academic performance. SN provides Internet-based products, supports, and services to partner districts in order to facilitate data and information access for teachers, administrators, and the community.[8]

SN offers the ability to streamline district data systems and content with products that can accommodate and integrate other district initiatives under its umbrella. The computer modules are designed to be user-friendly and can be tailored to meet the needs of a broad cross-section of district and school staff, including teachers, principals, counselors, and district administrators.

A partnership begins when SN is contacted by a district staff person. SN does not require buy-in from any particular district or school staff members; however, the contractual nature of the partnership between SN and a district requires senior district officials to approve the partnership. In this partnership, the district office is the primary point of contact for SN and is typically the recipient of direct services. The partnering district selects particular SN products and services to lease or purchase, which often are customized for the district, and then the central office determines to whom, when, and how the data system will be introduced and used. SN serves as a supporting partner and advisor in these decisions and the subsequent implementation. SN leaves most, if not all, school-level implementation decisions up to the district.

The school district determines the scope of supports to be provided separately or in combination by SN, the district, or a third party. SN offers a range of services that are tailored to support the development and use of the system created for a district. These include an implementation framework, technological support, and capacity-building support through various forms of professional development. Technical assistance can include services such as data loading, hosting the district's Internet-based SN modules, and integrating existing programs into the SN system. With regard to training, SN typically offers a brief workshop for a subset of district staff and school-level representatives identified by the district. Armed with SN reference materials, these individuals then train school-based colleagues and serve as on-site resources. The underlying assumption in this approach is that if district staff are properly trained in the use of SN products, they will be able to pass that expertise along to school staff, who in turn will pass it along to teachers. Districts also can purchase other support from SchoolNet, including workshops and refresher sessions, site visits, on-site support days, and on-line assistance for all teachers and staff.

Enactment

Awareness of the reform, training, and support to foster SN use varied within each district.[9] District administrators who worked closely with SN representatives were the most aware of, and had extensive knowledge about, what the system could do and how SN fit into district priorities and ongoing work. School-level staff who received training either directly from SN or from district reform leaders were in the middle in terms of knowledge about SN. These school-based individuals often served as turnkey trainers and on-site advisors. The lowest level of awareness was held by the teachers at each school who were trained by the turnkey trainers. These teachers had the least exposure and preparation to use SN and usually represented the majority of teachers.

Of the SN modules available, each district, at a minimum, leased and provided school staff access to the module (Account) that tracks student performance and other data, allowing data to be examined at the school, student group, and individual levels. Other modules purchased were at varying stages of implementation in different schools within each district.

Across all three study schools, a majority of teachers were not involved in the implementation of SN, and teacher use, particularly when not mandated, was relatively low. One variation noted at two schools was that some teachers accessed SN directly, while others relied on school administrators to generate paper copies of SN reports, which they then reviewed. In the second year of this study, SN use was moving in opposite directions at the two early-implementing schools. At SN2, growing dissatisfaction with SN as a result of leadership changes and persistent problems obtaining accurate, timely data led teachers to use the system less and less. At SN1, SN use appeared to increase. This was attributed in large part to district requirements that teachers in the core content areas complete benchmark reports using SN-generated data. The core content areas include English, math, and science. Benchmark reports using SN-generated data were not required in social studies. The district used a different benchmark assessment system for this content area.

The three district offices coordinated professional development offerings for their respective schools. Initially, all three districts in the study relied on a turnkey training model to prepare teachers to use the SN modules. In each case, the district identified teams of teachers, department chairs, and/or administrators from each school to receive SN training so that they in turn would train teachers at their respective schools. At all three schools, members of the team designated to become school-based trainers explained that they did not receive sufficient training to carry out this task. To supplement the turnkey training, districts also offered a myriad of other professional development opportunities to support trainers and teacher use of SN. In some cases this included district-led SN workshops.

SN monitored implementation and use at the district level through regular communication with district office staff. SN staff had limited, if any, direct contact with teachers at the three schools. The three districts monitored SN use with varying consistency through user log-in reports and an assortment of other approaches. The most rigorous monitoring of SN use was by the SN1 district, which required school staff to complete benchmark reports.

Perceived Effects

Teacher and administrator understanding of SN varied significantly across the three schools. With the exception of one school administrator, school-level staff did not seem to have a complete understanding of all that SN offered or how the modules related to one another. There was a striking disparity in the overall value district and school staff placed on SN. District staff were enthusiastic about the reform, valuing the SN system's capacity to link data use to instructional planning and to provide access directly to teachers via the Internet. In contrast, school staff members were more often ambivalent or critical of SN and its capacity to facilitate their work. This lower level of support for the reform at the school level was evident despite a generally favorable predisposition to data-driven instruction, at least in theory.

Teacher reports suggest that SN stimulated few changes in teacher practice, and less than 35% of teachers at each school believed using SN required them to make major changes in their classroom practice. There was some evidence that SN supported changes in practice for department chairs, assistant principals, or others charged with accessing, organizing, and distributing data to teachers. In these cases it appeared that improved access helped them become more focused on data and better able to share data with teachers. In addition, there was some evidence that SN may have had a greater impact on district staff practice. For example, there reportedly was increased collaboration between the technology department and the curriculum and instruction department, and a collective focus on data collection and analysis linked to instructional goals. There were few instances in which school-level staff believed SN had an impact on student behavior or performance, which is not surprising given the low level of SN use at each of the three schools.

On its own, SN did not generate widespread enthusiasm among the teachers interviewed and surveyed at the three schools. Sustainability of the program was in question at all schools. For example, some SN1 teachers saw the reform "dying out after a while," while others believed the initiative would be sustained. By year two of this study, SN2 teachers and administrators did not believe SN would be sustained. Across the three schools, it was believed that district leadership commitment and the extent to which SN had become embedded in district operations were critical contributors to the reform's sustainability. Some noted that evidence of positive changes in student performance also would be important to continued leadership support and the reform's future.

VARIATION IN REFORM ENACTMENT ACROSS SCHOOLS

As illustrated in the case studies, we found substantial variation in both enactment and perceived effects of the five reforms. Variation was as great within the reforms as across them in many cases. Which elements of a reform were used, how they were used, the extent to which they were used, and the perceived effects varied enormously among schools using the "same" reform.

Reform enactment across schools was characterized by three types of variation that often overlapped or existed concurrently. First, schools and districts reinterpreted or modified the reforms that were intended by the providers, making sense of them in the context of local policy, other reforms, and their own practice. Second, schools and districts differed in the degree of progress made in implementing even their own versions of the reforms. Finally, we found variation in the extent to which reforms reportedly affected teacher behavior and practice in the classroom, even within the same school.

As a result of district- and school-level reinterpretation of the reforms, the local versions were often quite different from the provider-intended reforms and from one another. In HSTW schools, for example, some reform components assumed greater importance than others, depending on local context. HSTW1 chose to focus on increasing graduation requirements and creating a student advisory program, while HSTW2 concentrated on creating grade-level academies, with specific emphasis on ninth grade. And while all three schools created some type of decision-making body, the way in which they did so was influenced by local factors. HSTW1 and HSTW3 adhered more closely to the HSTW focus team model, in which different teams address different areas of reform. At HSTW2, the teams, called "professional learning communities," were grade-level rather than topic-specific, in accordance with other reforms being implemented in the school. In SN schools, enactment was shaped by district goals and capacity. The provider focused on forming a partnership with the district, which in turn developed a roll-out strategy for the schools. As a result, school-level enactment—technology access, professional development, organizational supports, and expectations for use—varied by district.

While it can be argued that such local variation is to be expected from the HSTW and SN reform designs (see Chapter 3, this volume), we also found that in some schools the scope of reform—who in the schools was to be involved and to what end—varied considerably, and clearly departed from the provider-intended reform designs. In PLN3 and RU2, for example, reforms that were designed to focus initially on a small group of teachers were expanded to include the entire school. This required changes not only in the way the schools made sense of the reforms, but in the organizational supports required to enact the modified versions of the reforms. Conversely, HSTW2 seemed to engage small subsets of teachers, with broader faculty participation at a more superficial level. The limited teacher engagement at HSTW2 was at odds with the underlying philosophy of HSTW as a whole-school reform.

Turning to the second type of variation, schools and districts varied in the progress they made in implementation during the study period. This variation was particularly apparent in the enactment of structural reform components. Across most of the reforms there were individual schools where reform implementation appeared to be stalled. At SN3, teacher awareness and use of SN was very low, despite strong support at the district level. At FTF2, SLCs were adopted, but implementation of the family advocacy system and the instructional components was limited. At PLN1, the school opted not to partner with PLN after the first year of this study, primarily because the number of teachers interested in taking PLN courses was limited. On the other hand, some schools appeared to make substantial progress in implementing reform components. At FTF3, SLCs functioned autonomously, with professional development around instructional components delivered by SLC coordinators. At RU1, with district support, use and knowledge of the program were growing.

Finally, variation was reported in the extent to which the reforms affected teacher behavior and practice in the classroom. It is important to note that the reforms themselves varied considerably with regard to how they tried to affect teacher behavior and practice, and that this study was not designed to capture actual (as opposed to self-reported) changes in instruction. That said, teacher reports suggest variation in the adoption of instructional practices. Participating teachers at the three PLN schools varied in the degree to which they thought PLN expected them to alter their teaching practice; most stated that they used a PLN strategy as an "add-in" when it fit. At the RU schools, some RU teachers suggested that the reform required a lot of changes to their teaching practice, while others reported that the reform merely rearranged many things that they already had been doing. Additionally, both PLN and RU teachers tended to use techniques that were more familiar to them and that aligned with their current teaching practice, and were less likely to use strategies that significantly challenged or altered it. Similarly, some HSTW teachers suggested that the reform had changed their practice completely, suggesting that they held students to higher standards, took more responsibility for students' success, and worked more collaboratively than others. Other teachers suggested that HSTW offered some useful "tricks" that could be added to their existing repertoire, but did not require them to make major changes in practice. Relatively few teachers at any of the SN schools reported that the reform required them to make major changes in their practice, but here too reported use of the reform among teachers varied both across and within schools.

In sum, implementation of the five reforms varied greatly across the 15 schools in this study. This variation was evident in both the ways that the reforms were interpreted and the progress that schools and teachers made in adopting reform components and practices. The chapters that follow explore several factors that help to explain the variation in implementation that we observed.

NOTES

1. The case studies presented in this chapter are summaries of more detailed cases prepared as part of our analysis. The full versions of the case studies are available on the CPRE website at www.cpre.org.

2. The high schools in this study range from early implementers to mature schools. As explained in Chapter 1, after the provider abbreviation, the number 1 denotes a school that was in its first year of implementation, the number 2 a school that was in its second year of implementation, and the number 3 a school that had been implementing for 3–5 years.

3. Demographic information about the three FTF schools can be found in the Appendix, Table A.1. In brief, all three FTF schools were large high schools (1,000–2,000 students). Two schools (FTF2 and FTF3) were located in large urban school districts characterized by a long history of low student performance. At the time that they partnered with FTF, both of these high schools had a history of missing state and federal performance targets, although FTF3 did meet federal adequate yearly progress (AYP) standards for the 2005–06 school year, suggesting an improvement in traditional performance. The other school (FTF1) had an ethnically diverse student body (60% students of color, 40% White) and, unlike the other schools, at the time of its partnership with FTF, it missed AYP due only to subgroup performance.

4. Because AC and RU share some techniques and structural elements, it was often hard for interviewees to distinguish one from the other.

5. One of these taught RU at the middle school level; there was only one RU teacher for the high school.

6. Also, in 2005, PLN entered into a partnership with the Annenberg Foundation to help lead the Pennsylvania High School Coaching Initiative, a 3-year $30 million project to supply math and literacy instructional leadership training and coaching to at least 10 "high need" schools and school districts in Pennsylvania (see http://www.pacoaching.org/). It is possible that this project and future involvement in other ventures may reshape the way PLN traditionally has operated.

7. For the survey, participating teachers at PLN1 and PLN2 are those who took a PLN course, about five or six teachers for each survey administration. At PLN3, survey data are based on all survey respondents. The reason for looking only at the teachers who participated in PLN is to give an accurate picture of how teacher behavior and instructional practice were impacted by PLN.

8. As of the 2004–05 study period, some of the Internet-based products (or modules) available for lease individually or in combination from SN included Account (tracks student performance data), Align (enables districts to align and disseminate curriculum, instruction, and assessment), Assess (centralizes and automates the processes for benchmark tests and can align test items with state

standards), Outreach (disseminates information about district and schools to the community via the Internet), and Data Warehouse (makes data available from disparate systems and warehouses readily available data). Modifications to SchoolNet modules are ongoing. For more information, see www.schoolnet.com.

9. Both SN2 and SN3 were based in communities transitioning from rural to suburban, and their student populations were becoming increasingly diverse. During the study, SN2 was in the midst of substantial changes in leadership, teaching staff, and student enrollment. At SN3, the district faced budget constraints and contended with the limitations of a small district office staff, and school staff described strained relations with the district office. Both schools met AYP in recent years, although some subgroups did not. In contrast, SN1 was based in a large urban district characterized by a long history of low student performance, high poverty, and management difficulties. The school had stable leadership over the previous several years, and its students were ethnically diverse and more than two thirds lived in poverty. SN1 did not make AYP and was in corrective action.

REFERENCES

Berends, M., Kirby, S. N., Naftel, S., & McKelvey, C. (2001). *Implementation and performance in New American Schools: Three years to scale-up*. Santa Monica, CA: RAND Corporation.

Connell, J. P. (2002). *Getting off the dime: First steps towards implementing First Things First*. Toms River, NJ: Institute for Research and Reform in Education.

Institute for Research and Reform in Education. (n.d.). *Planning year tasks and schedule*. Toms River, NJ: Author.

Southern Regional Education Board. (2005). *High Schools That Work: An enhanced design to get all students to standards*. Atlanta, GA: Author.

CHAPTER 3

Channeling Adaptation: The Role of Design in Enactment Patterns

Catherine Dunn Shiffman, Matthew Riggan, Diane Massell, Matthew Goldwasser, and Joy Anderson

High schools are under intense pressure to change the ways in which students are educated. Increasingly, schools and districts seek the assistance of external school reform organizations in such endeavors. In order to achieve the kinds of results intended with these substantial investments of public and private resources, there is a critical need to understand external school reform designs and how they are implemented in schools and districts. On the basis of decades of research, as reviewed in Chapter 1, we know that when external policies and programs enter a classroom, school, and district, they almost assuredly will be altered in some way by the individuals interpreting and enacting the design (Berends, Bodilly, & Kirby, 2002; Berman & McLaughlin, 1978; Datnow, Hubbard, & Mehan, 2002; Fullan, 1991). Datnow and colleagues contend that we have "underestimated the co-constructed nature of the implementation process" (p. 10).

In this chapter, we focus on characteristics of the designs themselves that influence the adaptation process. More specifically, we examine the role that program design played in the implementation of reform programs in 15 high schools. Four design factors were key in shaping a reform's propensity for modification by individuals in the study schools:

1. The *emphasis* of particular reform ideas, strategies, and practices embedded in the design
2. The *complexity* posed by the reform for teachers and administrators putting the design into place
3. The degree to which the design *engaged* teachers and administrators
4. The *implementation support* provided to facilitate enactment

These four design factors interacted with one another so that decisions made to address one design factor often influenced the range of possible choices related to the other three design factors. The influence of these factors was evident across the five designs included in the study: two whole-school reforms (High Schools That Work [HSTW] and First Things First [FTF]), two targeted literacy programs (Ramp-Up to Literacy [RU] and the Penn Literacy Network [PLN]), and one technology initiative to spur data use (SchoolNet [SN]).

Two themes permeated the degree to which local enactors were likely to modify elements in each of the design factors. First, the degree of specificity that accompanied implementation instructions determined what was left to the enacting school and district to interpret. Previous research suggests that where there is greater specificity, it is easier for enactors to understand what the design should look like and to assess the degree of fidelity achieved in implementation (Berends et al., 2002; Desimone, 2002). Yet some also have observed that greater specificity can constrain the conversation on the school side, and by association limit the opportunities for schools and individual educators to co-construct a design that reflects their particular context, needs, and strengths (Datnow et al., 2002; McLaughlin & Mitra, 2002). Greater design specificity also raises the potential for conflict with other mandates, efforts, and priorities that are simultaneously present in the school environment and are placing demands on teachers.

Second, interactions were evident among the four design factors as they were enacted in the study schools. Other researchers have noted this phenomenon as well, observing that decisions made in one design area could influence the range of "decisions and responses available in another category" (Glennan, Bodilly, Galegher, & Kerr, 2004, p. 31). Also, reform program providers that value locally constructed reforms often have had to contend with demands from teachers for specific instructions regarding how to enact the design (Desimone, 2002). In this study, such interactions were prevalent between design emphasis and the realities of engaging teachers and administrators in the reform within an environment of competing demands for staff and funding attention.

The reform program that is enacted can be conceptualized as a series of interactions among the design, the enacting school or district, and the external school reform organization. These dialogues are dynamic, fluid, and evolving. They also are infused with some tension between remaining true to key design components and goals of the reform, and addressing strong pressures to adapt the design to a specific local context. External school reforms are created by individuals who often have devoted years to developing and refining the designs based on their experiences as reform program providers, researchers, and educators. Thus, the design promoted by the provider is often grounded in strongly held beliefs about how the design can achieve the types of reform it seeks to address, and in substantial experience working with teachers, schools, and districts implementing the design. Yet in any given context, enacting teachers and administrators tend to adjust the design in ways that reflect their priorities, understanding, and capacities.

Following this introduction, we use the four design factors as a framework to explore patterns of reform program enactment and adaptation observed across the study schools. We found that those design components emphasized in the early stages of implementation and those central to core reform goals were more likely to be enacted in the study schools. Next, we explore the complexity particular design components posed for schools and teachers. We discuss two dimensions of this complexity: level of abstraction and degree of technical difficulty. We then discuss the types of engagement strategies designs employed that appeared more likely to garner teacher and leader attention and involvement. Commitment to and interest in the reform were strengthened when the problem addressed by the design was perceived as relevant and important, and when evidence of the design's effectiveness was observed. Finally, we examine the role of implementation supports in fostering enactment. We found that staff that had more direct contact with professional development, technical assistance, and supplemental supports articulated a greater understanding of the reform ideas and more often expressed their commitment to and involvement in the reform. As we discuss each factor, we point to interactions among the factors and the influence of specificity in guiding modifications. We conclude with implications of this design perspective for providers, schools, and districts.

Data for this chapter were drawn from interviews with provider staff, teachers, and school and district administrators. In addition, we reviewed printed materials available from the providers. Our analysis was conducted in several phases. We began by examining the designs as they were presented by the provider. Then we explored how the designs were enacted from the perspectives of provider, school, and district staff. We focused on interviewees' impressions of the design as it was originally intended by the provider and how it was enacted in schools and classrooms. We then looked across the 15 schools and five designs for enactment patterns that could be explained by the designs, and identified the four design factors.

It is important to keep in mind that the designs are not static. Rather, the providers continually revise their designs based on knowledge and experiences accumulated through implementing the reform in all of their schools and as research and technology evolve. This chapter considers the designs as they existed in the sample high schools during the study period. In addition, this chapter does not examine the ways in which the providers' organizational capacities, constraints, and priorities guided provider responses to adjustment pressures. Although this is an important dimension of understanding how, when, and why designs are revised, it is beyond the scope of the research.

DESIGN EMPHASIS

Designs inevitably emphasize certain components over others, and this prioritization is important in implementation (Bodilly, Keltner, Purnell, Reichardt, & Schuyler, 1998). These emphases originate in a design's theory of action regarding how the reform should unfold in schools. Two recurrent themes are embedded in a theory of action. The first concerns where the reform should be constructed. Designs may be "built" primarily in the offices of the provider, in the school and/or the district office, or some combination (Desimone, 2002; Glennan et al., 2004; Kronley & Handley, 2003). The location of that development work reflects core philosophical beliefs about reform ownership and the relevance of local context. Some reforms, for example, are premised on the notion that authority must be decentralized and reform ideas reinterpreted locally (Muncey & McQuillan, 1996). This decision about where reforms are to be located also reflects strategic choices regarding what will facilitate, as effectively as possible, deep and sustained use of the reform. Some propose that the way to garner buy-in is to deeply steep educators in the philosophy and core principles of an approach at the outset, even prior to action in the school or classroom (McLaughlin & Mitra, 2002). Others suggest that understanding and motivation will be built as implementation leads to positive changes in the school (Connell, 2002).

The second theme that guides what designs prioritize is the role that schools' organizational conditions play in facilitating the changes called for in the reform. Some designs rely on particular groupings of students and teachers, divisions of authority, or class scheduling as preconditions to instructional change. Other designs focus on individual teachers and their classroom practice, relegating organizational conditions to the backseat or ignoring them altogether. This second theme reflects beliefs about how individual practice is connected to or can be dissociated from the organization of schooling. It also reflects strategic choices regarding the efficiency with which change can be enacted—and, in many cases, enacted broadly throughout a school—in an environment where priorities shift and leader and staff turnover is an ever-present possibility. These beliefs and strategies influence decisions about which features of the design to prioritize, and in what sequence. We turn now to examine how the sequence and centrality of the design components were associated with enactment and use of these components in the study schools.

Sequencing

During the study period, schools were more likely to enact the design components that were emphasized first. The attention and resources of both the provider and school and district actors were most focused on the reform at the early stages. Furthermore, these early components often were more fully elaborated or specified as to what teachers and district or school leaders should do.

When the design called for teachers and leaders to immediately incorporate prescribed design activities into their practice, these were the activities we were likely to see enacted in the study schools. For example, the FTF design expected teachers to begin by restructuring the school into small learning communities (SLCs). Resources and attention of the provider and the school were heavily concentrated on putting the SLC structure in place and were accompanied by detailed recommendations for student–teacher ratios, SLC themes, and student groupings. The RU design also began with a specified set of instructions, in this case for pedagogy, curriculum, and classroom arrangements for teachers. We found that RU teachers were, in fact, enacting many of the curriculum and classroom specifications early in the school year.

In contrast, the HSTW and PLN designs focused efforts on building commitment through a process of understanding and experimenting with the reform ideas and co-constructing plans for translating these reform ideas into practice. These designs began with a focus on fitting the design to the problem or needs identified by local enactors. During the study period, we found that the focus of resources and attention in HSTW schools was oriented toward problem definition and planning steps for improvement, and in the PLN schools toward experimenting with techniques and approaches. For SN, the locus of development was at the district office. Here, the providers concentrated resources and attention on their partnership with the district, while the schools received less attention or design-related resources in the early years of implementation. As a result, we found that implementation was well underway in the district offices but not at the three schools.

During the study period, the designs focused to different degrees on the roles of organizational structures to support the reforms. The relative focus on structures and instruction guided the sequence of changes. Consequently, we observed that when structures were focused on first, they were more fully enacted in the study schools. The two whole-school designs required extensive alterations in school organization or governance before any significant changes in teaching practice were undertaken. We observed that these structures were largely in place in the schools, while changes in instructional practice were still in the early stages or, in some cases, had yet to take hold. In contrast, while the RU and PLN designs did call for some structural conditions, the focus of these two targeted literacy initiatives was on changing what happens in the classroom around literacy instruction. The lesser emphasis on structural changes in the design was communicated to teachers by less provider attention and support to make the structural changes. Thus, the designs left it to the schools and their leaders to determine how to arrange a block schedule or the time for teachers to experiment with new ideas. While teachers reported using the literacy programs' instructional and curricular design elements in these schools, we found wider variation in the extent to which leaders had developed the supporting structures.

Given this study's general emphasis on the early phase of implementation, it is logical—and likely reassuring to providers and schools—that what was called for in the early years of implementation was reported to be in place. These early years were of particular importance for the reforms' future in the schools. First, the reforms typically were planned (and funded) for only brief periods of time, ranging from months to a few years. In our sample, we found evidence in some schools and districts that attention and resources were being shifted away from the reform, leaving its future somewhat questionable. Second, given that these reforms were implemented in shifting contexts, other research suggests that we should pay particular attention to what is implemented in the early years (Barnes, Khorsheed, de Los Rios, & Correnti, 2006; Vernez, Karam, Mariano, & DeMartini, 2004). Vernez and his colleagues found that the time a school had used a comprehensive school reform model "did not appear to be related to the degree to which its various requirements were actually implemented after the model had been in use for one to two years" (p. 67). In several cases, turnover in key leadership positions or changes in funding within the three-year study period signaled a weakening of the reform's prominence on the school's and district's agenda and, with it, waning commitment for continued implementation.

Centrality

Vernez and his colleagues (2004) observed that comprehensive school reform design components fell into two categories: "(1) core components . . . without which the model would lose its uniqueness or identity; and (2) support components that are designed to increase school staff capacity to implement the core components of the model" (p. 49). Similarly in this study, the designs tended to direct more resources and greater specificity to central features of the design and left the less central components to schools to enact on their own. For example, assistance from RU provider staff and supporting materials were focused largely on instructional changes. Less central, although desirable, features such as cross-age tutoring were left to schools to make happen. While we observed that the designs were adjusted in the study schools, providers also appeared more willing to negotiate about pieces of their design that were more peripheral rather than central principles. The central features often became evident when they were challenged by enactors. For example, the FTF design strongly rejected grouping students by ability. When a school considered an alternative to this, provider staff strongly objected, and additional staff time and materials were supplied to address school difficulties in creating and maintaining equitable SLCs.

At times, central design principles were in conflict with one another in the study schools, pointing to a hierarchy among those principles most central to the design. Providers adjusted some components to support others. For example, in some schools, the faculty-developed plans for improvement were viewed by the provider as insufficient to foster HSTW's 10 key practices for high schools. In particular, we saw the reform's focus on building high expectations for all students and a rigorous curriculum take precedence over bottom-up construction of school improvement.

COMPLEXITY

Enacting design components poses varying degrees of complexity for teachers and administrators. Complexity is defined as the difficulty local enactors encounter in the process of learning about and using a component, as well as the departure from current behavior that any given design component represents (Fullan, 1991; Mazmanian & Sabatier, 1983; Rogers, 1995). As local enactors encounter complexity, the chances for altering a design component expand, resulting in a range of interpretations and adaptations in schools and classrooms.

Research suggests that the complexity of design components is one factor that influences successful adoption of reforms. Drawing attention to the complexity associated with instructional change, Ball and Cohen (2003) argue that the "more novel the instructional design, the greater the distance from modal practice, the more crucial it is that the intervention take into account the complexity of instruction and its demands" (p. 19). Barnes and colleagues (2006) found that some of the more intricate instructional activities called for in the two whole-school designs they studied were not routine for teachers or their students. Furthermore, these components depended on teachers to elaborate or adapt them, and therefore required more time for teachers to learn how to use them, often more than two years.

Our analysis focused on two dimensions of complexity at work in the study schools' interaction with their selected design: the level of abstraction and the degree of technical difficulty. *Abstraction* refers to concepts in the designs that defy easy specification or translation into actionable implementation steps, while *technical difficulty* relates to the level of skill required in a particular area to complete a design component. In both cases, the higher the degree of complexity, the greater the likelihood of modification.

Level of Abstraction

All five designs represent efforts to translate abstract concepts into concrete design components so that enactment of the components results in the incorporation of the concepts. Yet many concepts defy the kind of clear definition that would make such a transformation possible. For example, nearly every reform (and all five in this study) professes the need to maintain "high expectations" for students. While expectations can be "encoded" into more concrete interventions such as standards, they also are reflected in the attitudes, behaviors, and communication strategies of individual teachers. These individual traits and practices are much more difficult to define and may or may not be influenced by the adoption of more concrete design components such as standards or curriculum.

Among the five designs in the study, three other abstract concepts presented similar "translation" problems. First, several designs sought to realize some version of "professional community"—a set of organizational and behavioral norms related to the interaction, communication, and co-construction of professional practice (Hargreaves & Fink, 2006). Yet the interventions designed to foster the emergence of such a community were often structural (e.g., scheduling meeting times or the creation of SLCs or other decision-making bodies). These components could be enacted without necessarily adopting the professional behaviors they sought to engender. In our research, we found evidence of such disconnects in schools implementing the FTF, HSTW, and PLN designs, each of which sought to foster professional community through enactment of specific design components.

Second, the concept of "rigor" proved vexing. Teachers were acutely aware that reforms required them to increase the rigor of their instruction, yet few were able to identify what that meant in concrete terms. Instead, rigor was interpreted personally and subjectively by most teachers. In some cases, rigor was considered tantamount to the design components that were meant to instill it, such as increasing graduation requirements. The idea of rigor as a principle that guided instructional practice was much more difficult to encode into the designs.

Third, "student engagement" was a critical component for most of the designs. The designs sought to engage students in various ways, including the establishment of SLCs to improve relationships between teachers and students (FTF), adoption of instructional practices to build on student successes (RU), and the implementation of advisory systems to better connect students, parents, and teachers (FTF and HSTW). In each case, the introduction of design components was intended to better engage students, resulting in a deeper commitment to school, greater effort, and improved outcomes. Again, however, engagement proved to be a largely affective and subjective quality. Teachers worked hard to engage students, but their success in doing so was not necessarily coupled with design components that were aimed to facilitate the process.

The goal is to embed reform ideas into practice in such a way that adoption of design components leads to, or coincides with, understanding and incorporation of those ideas. The risk is that enactors may adopt components procedurally without fully understanding or embracing the foundational concepts. All five designs struggled with the challenge of encoding abstract concepts such as professional community, rigor, and relationships into tangible guidance for ongoing teacher practice.

Level of Technical Difficulty

Design components that are clearly defined and communicated may still prove subject to modification if their successful adoption requires a high level of technical skill. Such difficulty was evident in all five designs. The RU design, for example, is highly specific and supported with extensive materials and professional development. Yet fully enacting certain components requires a high level of technical sophistication. At an administrative level, cross-age tutoring requires coordinating teaching schedules, faculty, and students. In the classroom, individualized reading assessments and conferencing require both expertise in literacy instruction and classroom management. Not surprisingly, these components were among the least implemented in the three schools using RU.

Data use is another area in which technical difficulty appeared to influence use. At the SN schools, for instance, accessing student performance data online required a basic level of computer proficiency to navigate the SN web portal. Teachers who lacked these basic skills frequently asked others to access data for them, resulting in a modification in how SchoolNet was used. Analyzing data to inform instruction through practices such as flexible grouping or alternative teaching strategies was another skill area in which degree of difficulty appeared to limit use.

Whether abstract or technically difficult, complex ideas and instructional practices were more likely to be enacted in ways consistent with the design when they were accompanied by extensive supports from the provider and school and district leaders. To assist schools in implementing technically difficult design components, providers offered increased support in the form of technical assistance, mentoring, site visits, monitoring, and additional training. Abstract concepts left greater elaboration to teachers and administrators and, therefore, resulted in a broader interpretive range. In some cases this undermined the potency of a particular design component in supporting core reform goals.

ENGAGEMENT OF TEACHERS AND ADMINISTRATORS

The five designs assumed different approaches to engaging teachers and school and district administrators. Broadly, these efforts focused on ensuring commitment as a necessary condition for implementation, gaining commitment through the process of co-constructing the reform, and/or involving teachers and administrators immediately in the design activities and structures under the premise that commitment would emerge as these local actors experienced success and found value in the reform. Reforms were more or less successful in building commitment of teachers and leaders when at least one of three dynamics was at work:

- Teachers and leaders viewed the design or a particular design component as central to their work
- The design or a component addressed a problem the teacher or school leader also considered a problem

- Teachers and leaders could witness evidence of a design component's effectiveness in their work

Commitment as a Condition of Participation and Through Co-construction of the Reform

While all of the designs reflected a belief in building teacher commitment to engage in and learn about their reform ideas in meaningful ways, commitment was sought through different strategies, reflecting a split in the literature. The HSTW and PLN designs sought teacher commitment as a condition of participation. Both designs also devoted time in the initial stages to deep exposure and conversation about the reform ideas, an approach supported by some researchers (e.g., McLaughlin & Mitra, 2002). The designs were structured to give teachers the opportunity to adapt the reform to the needs of their school or classroom context. In this scenario, professional commitment was expected to emerge as teachers refined ideas to fit their context.

The HSTW design also called for shifting some authority to teachers by first requiring their consent to adopt the reform into the school, and then by requesting them to develop goals and plans for improvement. We found, however, that the adoption and planning processes were subject to modification when teacher-led decisions were inconsistent with the goals of school leaders or provider staff. The initial faculty vote was compromised at one early-adopting school by a voting process in which many faculty members believed they were signing an attendance sheet rather than casting a vote for the reform. At the other early-adopting school, a new principal was hired with the expectation of enacting HSTW before teacher input had even been solicited. In both early-adopting schools we also observed that while the design planned time for faculty to collectively explore the reform ideas and build consensus around a school improvement plan, many faculty members had a sense that the reform was being shaped and directed by administrators or provider staff.

Like HSTW, the traditional PLN design, in which a course was offered to teachers, assumed teacher commitment as a condition of participation because teachers volunteered to enroll in the class. At the two early-adopting schools this voluntary approach to participation was clear to teachers. Teachers had to make concerted efforts to enroll, attend the course during the school year, and secure available reimbursement and certification credit. Thus, the reform's prospects for continuation were highly susceptible to individual, school, and district contextual factors. At the two early-adopting schools, insufficient interest (attributed to a range of factors, including teacher reimbursement mechanisms and certification needs) led the districts to scale down or eliminate the courses offered by the reform.

Engagement Through Altering Teachers' and Leaders' Work Lives

When the reform intruded on teachers' work in some way, teachers were more apt to become engaged. These intrusions could involve the organization of teachers' school day, classroom instruction, or relationships with colleagues and students. The FTF design called for restructuring the school into theme-based SLCs and implementing a family advocacy system. Both of these changes altered teachers' experiences as instructors, as colleagues, and as guides to their students. They had no choice but to engage in certain components of the design. The HSTW design expected faculty to join focus teams to identify goals for the school. Here, we observed differences in engagement levels based on the degree of centrality (as described in the previous section) of a particular focus team's work to the reform. Those focus teams charged with implementing high-priority components were, not surprisingly, more engaged.

In other cases involvement was secured through mandated use of the reform in teachers' routine work. When teachers in the three SN schools were required to use the data management system in their work, they became engaged at least on a superficial level. Where such requirements were absent, teachers largely did not access the system. For example, when one district required teachers in the core subject areas to use SN-generated data to analyze and report on student progress, a requirement reinforced by the principal, these teachers used the system. Those teachers not teaching in core subject areas were less apt to use the SN system, and the core teachers limited their SN use to the mandated task.

Related to this, we observed that the individuals directly engaged in implementing core design components expressed greater understanding of and commitment to the reform. This was strikingly apparent in the divergent opinions about SN's value between those district administrators intimately engaged in planning and implementing the SN system and those school administrators and teachers who had little or no role.

The designs engaged formal leaders in implementation in different capacities. We define formal leaders as individuals who hold administrative leadership positions within schools (e.g., principal, assistant principal, department chair). Where formal leaders were central to implementation, we saw more engagement in the form of either supporting or actively modifying the design to meet the goals for the school. The PLN design did not require the creation of any new leadership positions within the school.

And while principals were encouraged to participate in staff development, they were not required to take on any specific tasks related to implementation, either at the school or classroom level. In the two early-adopting schools these leaders were largely uninvolved in implementing PLN. On the other hand, the FTF and HSTW designs called for the principal to play a central role in implementing the reform, whether in terms of organizing school resources, participating in professional development, or creating pressure for change in the school. These designs also anchored the implementation of their designs to the creation of new leadership positions.

In addition, the designs varied in their efforts to engage leaders to assume instructional leadership roles. The RU design recommended that both a supervisor and literacy coach play an active instructional role. While the principal was not explicitly assigned an instructional role in the Ramp-Up design, the supervisor role often was enacted by a principal or assistant principal. The supervisor was expected to use performance data to identify students for enrollment in RU classes and to monitor progress, while the literacy coach provided support for RU teachers who already had received training from the provider. The RU design, accompanied by detailed instructions, required teachers to alter their classroom practice dramatically and immediately. From the first day of an RU class, teachers were expected to follow a detailed plan for instruction that required altering every aspect of their daily work. In addition to a new curriculum, these teachers used new RU instructional strategies, as well as classroom arrangements and materials. Teachers involved in RU were actively engaged in following the RU program for raising student literacy levels.

By contrast, instructional leadership responsibilities were less well-defined in the SN and PLN designs. SN clearly assumed that principals and department heads used student performance data to make decisions about curriculum, instruction, and professional development. And while the PLN design did not identify a specific role for principals, provider staff indicated that in cases where the reform was most successful, principals were engaged in deep conversations about instruction with teachers and understood the reform's role in improving teaching and learning.

Engagement Through Shared Perceptions of the Problem

To engage teachers and leaders on a deeper level than simple compliance, the problem the design sought to address needed to resonate with teachers. We observed more interest among teachers and administrators when a problem identified by a design echoed their own concerns. In this study, the design strategies that focused on increasing student engagement in academic work generated a lot of interest among teachers. The FTF design introduced student engagement strategies during the planning year in part as a strategy to build teacher interest when much of the reform's details were still an abstraction.

When the problem addressed by the design did not correspond to teacher or school leader priorities, additional efforts were needed to successfully engage teachers. In the RU schools, administrators found that some English teachers did not believe that basic reading skills were their responsibility to address; hence, for these individuals, addressing literacy needs was not a priority. The extent to which teachers were able to recognize literacy as their responsibility was considered a key stepping stone to garnering teachers' interest and engagement in the reform.

An extension of this was the perception that the design offered an appropriate solution to the problem as it was defined by teachers and leaders. Whether the design was viewed as an appropriate solution was dependent to some extent on the way in which teachers believed the problem could be solved most efficiently. While leaders and teachers in the SN schools agreed that analyzing student data to inform instructional and curricular decisions was important and worthwhile, what data-driven decision making actually entailed was less clear in our conversations with teachers. This was particularly true in two of the three SN sites. In these two sites, many teachers remained unconvinced that using the SN system was an efficient or necessary step in evaluating student performance and future planning.

Engagement Through Perceived Effectiveness

Finally, interest in the reform and particular components was strengthened when teachers were able to witness some evidence of success using a particular design strategy or activity. As one FTF representative noted, "[Teachers] need to see success." The designs' student engagement components lent some support for this statement. Both teachers and provider staff frequently cited the designs' student engagement components as those most successfully implemented and as having particular value to teachers. The FTF design offered relatively straightforward engagement components that were easy to implement in the classroom, and teachers were able to quickly observe positive changes in student attitudes. As referenced in the previous section, this was a strategic decision on the part of FTF's developers to increase teacher engagement during the planning year.

RU teachers and school and district administrators pointed to increased reading and interest in books among RU students as evidence that they were achieving some success in engaging students in ways that supported literacy development. "Almost universally teachers and kids report back being more engaged in Ramp-Up than they are in their other classes. And this engagement has been transformative for a lot of kids, and for a lot of teachers" (RU provider representative). Teachers, having seen the change in students, felt increasingly committed to the reform.

IMPLEMENTATION SUPPORT AND MONITORING

The fourth design factor guiding school- and teacher-level modification is the provision of implementation support. Supports identified in prior research as helping to foster implementation include

- Teacher training that is grounded, specific, and extensive
- Assistance that is classroom-based
- Communication directly with a provider staff member or reform leader
- Common planning time
- The local development of project material (Berends et al., 2002; Bodilly, 2001; McLaughlin & Mitra, 2002; Slavin, 2004)

Frequent opportunities to work with the same or similar ideas and content over time on material that is embedded in teachers' and administrators' work is one of the more effective approaches to professional learning. Furthermore, on-site learning with a skilled practitioner or teacher-leader provides opportunities for ongoing learning. Yet such supports are labor- and resource-intensive for both the provider and the school. Staff support, in particular, may fall short of what is recommended or needed (Barnes et al., 2006; Vernez et al., 2004). The full costs of the reform effort in terms of resources and staff time are also very difficult to anticipate at the time the partnership is initiated between the provider and the school or district (Hatch, 2002). While providers generally are increasing services, assistance, and monitoring (Berends et al., 2002), the capacity of the providers or the implementing schools to fund or supply those additional supports was often in question in the study schools.

Professional development, materials, and technical assistance found in the five designs varied in reach, specificity, and responsiveness to changing needs over time. The variation could be attributed to decisions related to other design factors (e.g., emphasis, complexity, engagement strategies) and the reality that resources available to implement the design were often limited. Embedded in the designs were decisions about who (e.g., consultants, provider staff, or school- or district-based staff) transmitted reform knowledge to teachers and in what location, the frequency and duration of any training, and the continuity of that training over time. Turnkey training, in which a teacher or other school leader received training and then shared that learning with school colleagues, was used to varying extents in the designs. While this method of communicating reform ideas is typically efficient and cost-effective, it poses challenges for communicating deep knowledge of the reform to teachers unless the trainers themselves are well-versed in the reform and are given the time and resources needed to work with and motivate their colleagues.

We observed three characteristics of the supports provided to the study schools that were associated with teacher reports of their understanding and use of particular design components. First, individuals who had more frequent direct contact with provider staff and more opportunities to work with the reform tended to articulate a better understanding of the design and expressed stronger commitment to the reform. Second, and related to the first point, when provider staff had more contact with enacting teachers, particularly in the classroom, the provider staff had greater knowledge of progress toward implementation and could identify specific ways to encourage and support program use. Third, supplemental supports beyond those services arranged at the outset of the partnership between the provider and school/district often filled critical needs for assistance once implementation was underway.

Access to Provider Staff and Materials

Provisions for professional development varied substantially across the five designs in terms of opportunities for direct instruction from provider staff, classroom-based assistance in enacting the reform through monitoring and other observations, and supporting materials. In particular, when the designs relied heavily on turnkey approaches to communicating reform ideas to teachers, as opposed to direct provider support, teachers described greater confusion about the design components and how to use them in their work. SN initially was introduced to the majority of high school teachers in this study through brief sessions led by turnkey trainers who themselves described not feeling well-prepared for their roles as trainers and on-site resources. In contrast, the school and district staff who received additional training that was focused on tasks related to their job, and had contact with the provider, voiced greater confidence in their understanding of and ability to use the SN system. When other designs in the study offered turnkey training, it was done in conjunction with other supports, including direct training from provider staff, materials, and in some cases opportunities for provider staff or school leaders to observe and assist classroom-based use of the reform. FTF also used a turnkey training method to communicate information about the reform, but this training was offered in conjunction with training directly from provider staff, detailed materials, and guidance for observing and monitoring classroom-level implementation. In addition, provider staff periodically observed classroom practice and SLC meetings and led trainings.

The timing of professional development also could influence the intensity of exposure teachers received. For teachers introduced to the reform when it was first initiated, provider and school- or district-level resources were often most concentrated. Teachers also had more opportunities to collectively wrestle with the reform ideas and begin the process of adapting them to their school context. As time passed, teachers new to the reform received a second tier of training that was more likely to already have been modified through its initial adaptation. For example, teachers received RU training directly from provider staff for the length of the two-year contract, after which district staff took over this role. In one district, the district office had staff available who had undergone a rigorous certification process offered by the provider. In another district, RU professional development around the reform was intensive, but increasingly reflected district priorities. Teachers in other subjects were exposed to and encouraged to adapt RU ideas to their subject matter, and a writing component was integrated into the training and supporting materials as well. Staff turnover could further widen the range of teacher experiences with provider-led training. Here again, we observed tiers of training based on the extent to which teachers' tenure at the school coincided with the reform's introduction. For instance, widespread staff turnover in one FTF school resulted in generations of teachers introduced to the reform with increasing distance from the initial experience.

The degree to which leaders were supported in their roles varied. The SN and PLN designs offered no specific guidance about the role of formal leaders. For the schools in our sample, neither design provided professional development around leadership, nor did provider materials address the role of principals or other formal leaders. As noted above, turnkey trainers themselves did not feel prepared to carry out their role in SN implementation in the schools. Other designs in the study were more proactive and explicit in their efforts to influence leadership practice. For example, RU and FTF used both professional development and print materials to explicitly define the role of formal leaders in implementing the design. Although each sought to effect change in different ways, both outlined the specific tasks to be undertaken by formal leaders in the implementation process. RU offered specific training for supervisors and literacy coaches, and published a supervisor's handbook that outlined the roles and responsibilities of both positions and provided a step-by-step guide to the curriculum. FTF offered a similar package of supports to a broad range of leaders. Principals, school improvement facilitators, and SLC coordinators all participated in professional development. Provider materials specified in great detail what was expected from each position, including implementation checklists and calendars, and explained the history and logic of FTF's approach to leadership.

Communication Between the Reform Organization and Enactors

Implementation prospects are believed to be strengthened with "consistent, clear, and frequent communication and assistance between design developers and schools, particularly teachers" (Berends et al., 2002, p. 149). As outlined in the five designs, communication between provider staff and the enacting teachers varied in terms of whom the provider communicated with, the frequency of that contact, and the instances in which provider staff observed the reforms' enactment in schools and individual classrooms. On the basis of these conditions, we found a range in provider knowledge of how reform ideas were translated into school and teacher practices. This is important to recognize because when providers were not familiar with school-level enactment, the role of supporting implementation was shifted to school and district implementers, who may or may not have had the resources, skills, and reform knowledge needed to foster deep change. This created more room for school and district enactors to interpret and adapt the design to individual classrooms and the school. Given the variability in interpretations regarding how to translate reform ideas into practice, teachers and school leaders may not recognize disparities between surface-level adoption and deep incorporation of reform ideas into teacher practice and school structures, without additional oversight and support to help steer them toward the reform's more challenging principles and practices.

As part of the basic reform package, three of the designs included few opportunities for provider staff to visit classrooms and observe how teachers were translating reform ideas into their instruction. In the two targeted literacy initiatives (PLN and RU), provider staff knowledge of implementation was gleaned from teacher accounts of their practice in provider-led training sessions. SN knowledge of implementation in the three study high schools was almost entirely filtered through the district office. While SN staff had frequent interactions with the district office, there were minimal opportunities to interact with the high school teachers or to observe how they used the SN system in their work. Teacher-initiated questions in two of the SN schools traveled through layers of district and SN staff to find an answer. In contrast, the two whole-school designs included a central role for a provider staff member in implementation as part of the basic reform package. FTF and HSTW staff members visited the schools regularly over time, met with teachers and staff, observed classrooms and staff meetings, and were in frequent communication. This regular contact enabled provider staff to develop a more robust understanding of the level of depth surrounding their reform at the individual teacher and organizational levels in the study schools.

Availability of Supplemental Supports

While all five designs offered a variety of supports, these ranged in the extent to which they were made available to the schools as part of the basic package or required additional fees from the school or district. These expanded supports often included additional professional development that addressed specific problems, technical assistance visits, mentoring, and call-in support. Supports that involved provider staff time were expensive. Schools varied broadly in their capacity and willingness to either fund provider supports beyond those agreed upon at the outset and/or to commit more of their own resources to fill in gaps. We found that where teachers and schools stumbled in enacting the reform, the presence of supplemental supports that addressed immediate needs played an important role in clarifying for teachers what the design was asking them to do and how they could work through their difficulties. In many cases this supplemental support involved bringing provider staff into the schools and classrooms or, at a minimum, expanding opportunities for direct communication. For example, during the first implementation year, one district agreed to fund additional FTF professional development when the teachers encountered difficulties—a move viewed by school staff as smoothing over a potential hurdle in adapting the reform's instructional components.

Provider staff interviewed were aware of adult learning needs and recognized the tension between recommending supports that exceeded the design and the appeal for schools of a less expensive option for reform. RAND researchers have argued that design teams need to be able to successfully market to districts the need for such supports (Berends et al., 2002). The RU design, for example, was created as a stand-alone reform for schools and districts that could not afford or did not wish to purchase the more expensive whole-school design, America's Choice, which included more extensive supports. Yet the need for ongoing support to implement RU was recognized. According to one RU staff person, "You absolutely need coaches and/or assistant principals who are going to monitor it, ultimately supervise it so that faithful implementation does take place, and take root." Such statements were common in conversations with provider staff, who were anxious to provide supplemental supports but found financing these supports an ongoing challenge.

CONCLUSION

In this chapter, we have argued that characteristics of the designs themselves channel the interaction among the design, the enacting school or district, and the provider. We contend that these dialogues are influenced by decisions made in four key areas of the design: design emphasis, level of complexity posed to enacting teachers and administrators, strategies for engagement, and implementation supports.

Our findings suggest that design components that are central to core reform goals and are introduced early in implementation may be more likely to be enacted in a manner consistent with the design intent. Resources and attention of both the provider and local enactors tend to be most concentrated on design components that are closely tied to core reform goals and are emphasized early in implementation. Although our research focused on the early years of implementation, other research (Vernez et al., 2004) and our own observations in the mature study schools suggest that decisions about what should be emphasized early in implementation should be selected strategically, given the strong possibility that school and district attention, funding, and other resources targeted at the reform will shift over time to address other priorities.

Design components also present varying degrees of complexity for implementing teachers and administrators. Providers are particularly challenged to encode abstract concepts such as professional community, rigor, and relationships into the designs. The degree to which these can be encoded into specified and concrete tasks is likely to influence the range of interpretations among local enactors. Design components also can require a high level of technical skill on the part of teachers or administrators. Such difficulties are apparent in creating and maintaining a design's structural requirements, using particular instructional strategies, and conducting data analysis. When such tasks prove too difficult for local enactors, there is a strong tendency by teachers and administrators to modify or ignore them. These findings point to the need for providers and schools or districts to offer adequate implementation support to enact the more complex components of the design or plan for the variation that likely will result.

Our findings suggest that engagement strategies are more likely to attract the attention of implementers when teachers and leaders view the design or a particular component as central to their work, the design or a component addresses a problem that teachers and administrators also identify, there are opportunities to observe positive effects of the design, and sufficient implementation supports are provided. The provision of adequate supports is also important in enabling providers and schools to focus on the design components emphasized and to assist teachers and administrators in interpreting complex concepts and tasks. Our research suggests that when enactors receive extensive implementation support, have direct contact with the provider, and receive supplemental assistance as needs arise, enactors will have a better grasp of what is being asked of them and the capacity to carry it out. Taken together these findings lend further evidence for the need to engage local enactors in meaningful ways and invest in appropriate levels of supports to foster use that reflects a deep understanding of the reform.

Themes of interaction and specificity recurred throughout our analysis of the designs and their influences on implementation in schools. Design factors often interact with one another. As a result, decisions made in one area can limit the range of possible decisions and negotiations available within other design factors. Decisions regarding the level of specificity that should accompany design components also influence the range of interpretations made by enacting teachers and administrators and the possibilities for modification. With greater specificity in the design, enactors have a clearer understanding of what the design should look like and awareness of modifications that are made.

In sum, we argue that designs vary in the degree to which they accommodate, encourage, or invite reinterpretation by schools and districts. Providers use a variety of strategies to minimize adaptation or modification. However, designs reflect choices about whether and when to employ particular approaches. Absent such strategies, district- and school-level actors are more likely to reinterpret and thus reshape designs through enactment. An examination of choices about what is emphasized in the design, the level of complexity posed to enacting teachers and administrators, the strategies for engagement, and implementation supports provided can illuminate points at which design modifications are more or less likely.

REFERENCES

Ball, D. L., & Cohen, D. K. (2003). *Instructional improvement and the problem of scale*. Unpublished manuscript, University of Michigan at Ann Arbor.

Barnes, C., Khorsheed, K., de Los Rios, D., & Correnti, R. (2006, April). *Learning by design: Developing the know-how to improve teaching and learning in high pov-*

erty schools. Paper presented at the annual meeting of the American Educational Research Association, San Francisco.

Berends, M., Bodilly, S., & Kirby, S. N. (2002). *Facing the challenges of whole-school reform: New American Schools after a decade*. Santa Monica, CA: RAND Corporation.

Berman, P., & McLaughlin, M. W. (1978). *Federal programs supporting educational change: Vol. VIII: Implementing and sustaining innovations*. Santa Monica, CA: RAND Corporation.

Bodilly, S. J. (2001). *New American Schools' concept of break the mold designs: How designs evolved and why*. Santa Monica, CA: RAND Corporation.

Bodilly, S. J., Keltner, B. R., Purnell, S. W., Reichardt, R., & Schuyler, G. (1998). *Lessons from New American Schools' scale-up phase: Prospects for bringing designs to multiple schools*. Santa Monica, CA: RAND Corporation.

Connell, J. P. (2002). *Getting off the dime: First steps towards implementing First Things First*. Toms River, NJ: Institute for Research and Reform in Education.

Datnow, A., Hubbard, L., & Mehan, H. (2002). *Extending educational reform: From one school to many*. London: RoutledgeFalmer.

Desimone, L. (2002). How can comprehensive school reform models be successfully implemented? *Review of Educational Research, 72*(3), 433–479.

Fullan, M. G. (1991). *The new meaning of educational change*. New York: Teachers College Press.

Glennan, T. K., Bodilly, S., Galegher, J. R., & Kerr, K. A. (2004). *Expanding the reach of education reforms: Perspectives from leaders in the scale-up of educational interventions*. Santa Monica, CA: RAND Corporation.

Hargreaves, A., & Fink, D. (2006). *Sustainable leadership*. San Francisco: Wiley.

Hatch, T. (2002). When improvement programs collide. *Phi Delta Kappan, 83*(8), 626–639.

Kronley, R. A., & Handley, C. (2003). *Reforming relationships: School districts, external organizations, and systemic change*. Providence, RI: Brown University, Annenberg Institute for School Reform.

Mazmanian, D. A., & Sabatier, P. A. (1983). *Implementation and public policy*. Glenview, IL: Scott Foresman.

McLaughlin, M. W., & Mitra, D. (2002). Theory-based change and change-based theory: Going deeper, going broader. *Journal of Educational Change, 2*(4), 301–323.

Muncey, D. E., & McQuillan, P. J. (1996). *Reform and resistance in schools and classrooms: An ethnographic view of the Coalition of Essential Schools*. New Haven, CT: Yale University Press.

Rogers, E. M. (1995). *Diffusion of innovations* (4th ed.). New York: Free Press.

Slavin, R. E. (2004). Built to last: Long-term maintenance of success for all. *Remedial and Special Education, 25*(1), 61–66.

Vernez, G., Karam, R., Mariano, L., & DeMartini, C. (2004). *Assessing the implementation of comprehensive school reform models* (Working Paper WR-162-EDU). Santa Monica, CA: RAND Corporation.

CHAPTER 4

Going with the Flow: Communication and Reform in High Schools

Elliot H. Weinbaum, Russell P. Cole, Michael J. Weiss, and Jonathan A. Supovitz

Enhancing the communal aspects of schooling is a key mechanism for educational improvement. Organizational groupings that allow for high levels of communication and social interaction around professional issues can encourage teachers to share their knowledge and expertise (DuFour, 1999; McLaughlin & Talbert, 2001). Such groupings are important because they support teachers' efforts to sustain change: "The presence of a supportive professional community of colleagues in the school . . . reinforces normative changes and provides continuing opportunities to learn" (Coburn, 2003, p. 6).

Communication is the cornerstone of building professional community. It plays a vital role in enabling sharing of information, establishing professional norms, building trust, and fostering the use and spread of reform. While individuals may learn new information or a new approach and theory in a traditional setting, social networks are required for the psychological support system that reduces the isolation of innovators and innovative groups and makes their efforts more sustainable and more likely to spread throughout the organization (Agapitova, 2003). Networks have been defined as "open structures, able to expand without limits, integrating new nodes as long as they share the same communication codes (for example, values or performance goals)" (Castells, 1996, p. 470).

The Implementation Gap: Understanding Reform in High Schools, edited by Jonathan A. Supovitz and Elliot H. Weinbaum.

Understanding networks has enabled us to understand how communication flows in an organization and can help to build community. In this chapter, we illustrate how communication is most quickly and dramatically shaped by changes to the structure of schools. The structures that are in place or introduced by reforms are highly correlated with communication patterns. And, in the case of schools implementing reform, growth in reform-related communication is generally related to improved attitudes about the reform and enhanced reform-related practice. This chapter provides a number of ways to examine professional communication in high schools and the variables that may impact it. We hope that it will stimulate many conversations about how to shape professional communication in meaningful ways.

The theoretical and practical information about new practices or objectives that is introduced when a new reform enters a school context is rarely sufficient to encourage innovation. Individuals expected to innovate need to be connected to networks that can provide the types of tacit information that is gained almost exclusively through experience and experimentation. While formal professional training clearly is needed, at least one report has argued that access to tacit knowledge from peers and colleagues may be necessary in order to fully understand and employ the codified knowledge shared in more formalized settings (Organisation for Economic Cooperation and Development, 2003). Brown and Duguid (1991) argue that networks of professionals essentially complete the body of knowledge needed to maintain practice. This is particularly true when the expected practice represents a departure from traditional practice.

To focus our examination of staff communication in high schools, we address the following research questions:

1. What do professional communication networks look like among staff members in high schools?
2. What organizational and individual characteristics are associated with particular communication patterns?
3. How do the particular strategies pursued by external school reform organizations influence professional communication?
4. How similar or different are patterns of communication about the reform compared with communication in traditional areas of professional practice?
5. What is the relationship between the communication patterns we find in high schools and staff members' attitudes about the reform?

RESEARCH QUESTIONS AND DESIGN

In our research we use a method called *social network analysis* to illustrate existing communication patterns in high schools engaged in various external school reforms and to assess the impacts of several variables, including the reforms themselves, on professional communities in high schools. We show how both organizational structures like small learning communities and social interactions and networks influence communication patterns in schools.

Data

In order to answer the research questions, we analyzed survey data collected at the 15 high schools in this study.[1] The survey instrument that was used to obtain data about the schoolwide communication networks included five network questions, three of which focused on traditional professional concerns for teachers, one on communication about the reform being studied, and one on friendship connections (see Table 4.1).

For four of the network questions, respondents were prompted to name the individuals from whom they sought advice in that area. The fifth network, friendship, was not an advice-seeking relationship. We

Table 4.1. Five networks.

Network Label	*Survey Question*	*Group*
Classroom management	To whom, in your school, have you turned for advice about classroom management during this school year?	Professional
Course content and planning	During this school year, to whom in your school have you gone for help in selecting and planning course content coverage and pacing?	Professional
Low-performing students	During this school year, to whom in your school have you turned for advice on strategies to assist low-performing students?	Professional
Provider	Please list the people inside or outside your school to whom you turned for advice in using [reform name] during this school year.	Provider
Friendship	During this school year, with whom among your colleagues at this school do you "hang out" and discuss family, home, and/or personal issues?	Friendship

loosely refer to all five networks as "communication networks." Under each question, there was space on the survey for respondents to list up to five names for each network.[2] Using the names indicated by each survey respondent, we were able to develop a graphic representation of the communication patterns in each school (see Figure 4.1). In these graphics, teachers are depicted as nodes (the small circles in Figure 4.1) and the presence of communication between two individuals is represented as links (lines connecting the nodes). Our communication patterns are advice-seeking connections, and therefore the links have arrows indicating the direction of the advice seeking. The entire network picture is called a sociogram. From an individual perspective, each individual (or ego) and his or her connections are an ego-network. Therefore, these graphics are essentially a collection of ego-networks. All of the ego-networks for a particular area of communication are combined to represent the network of communication within a school, and can be demonstrated graphically, as in Figure 4.1.

The survey also collected information about individual teacher attributes (e.g., classes taught, free periods, administrative positions) as well as measures of teacher attitudes and behaviors related to the reform. These data were used to assess the extent to which teachers felt positively disposed

Figure 4.1. Sample sociogram.

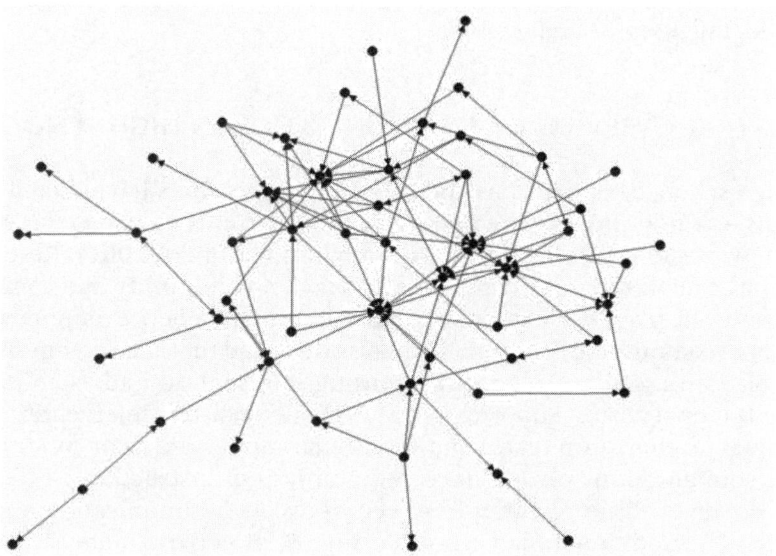

toward the reform and the extent to which they reported modifying their classroom practices in ways promoted by the reform in their schools.

Using these data, we were able to analyze advice-giving networks within a school. We did so using social network analysis, a method that quantitatively describes relationships among individuals in an organization. Furthermore, we were able to use familiar regression-like analyses to examine the associations between a variety of independent variables and the networks that are described in the data. (For a full explanation of the methods used, see van Duijn, Snijders, & Zijlstra, 2004.) Finally, we used the same data to examine the relationship between staff communication and the use of and attitudes about the reform.

Limitations

There are a few limitations to these analyses that must be acknowledged. First and foremost, the results obtained from our analyses are not causal. We were able to identify trends and associations between variables; however, the causal direction between variables could not be determined with our data. Second, for the purposes of network analysis, we imposed boundaries on the communication networks. We limited our networks to those within a given school. Although we recognize that sources external to schools are likely frequent sources of advice, we believe schools to be primary. Other research has identified schools as bounded organizations (e.g., Frank & Fahrbach, 1999), and we based our analysis on a similar belief. For this reason, conversations with individuals outside the schools were not included in our analyses.

GENERAL OVERVIEW OF COMMUNICATION IN HIGH SCHOOLS

In high schools, research has documented that teachers have established norms of autonomy that frequently prevent them from being connected to networks that may be of use (McLaughlin & Talbert, 2001). Research also has shown the important role that teacher community and communication can play. For example, McLaughlin and Talbert examined professional communities in 16 high schools and found that such communities can play an essential role in transmitting information and establishing organizational norms. Supovitz (2002) evaluated a district intervention that grouped teachers into teams and found that, under the right conditions, such configurations can produce communities of instructional practice.

However, little research has been done on communication among teachers in traditional high schools using social network analysis to describe and quantify relationships. In this section of the chapter, we will provide a general overview of communication networks in the 15 high schools surveyed. We first will focus on the amount and distribution of communication within the high schools. We then will look across the schools at which elements of traditionally organized high schools (e.g., academic departments, administrative positions) influence the likelihood that staff members will seek one another out for advice in areas of professional concern.

We analyzed advice-seeking communication around three familiar topics of professional concern for teachers: course content and planning, classroom management, and strategies for assisting low-performing students. These three professional communication networks were similar in specific ways: Within a given school the *total* amount of communication and the percentage of "isolated" teachers (those teachers who neither sought nor gave advice) were very consistent across the three professional networks. Essentially, within each school there was a similar number of total conversations occurring around each of these three areas and similar percentages of unconnected staff members. However, as we will discuss below, there were also clear differences among the three networks regarding the variables that predicted staff member communication in each of the networks.

Total Communication

Table 4.2 provides descriptive statistics for the three professional networks in each of the 15 high schools. The *mean out-degree* is a measure of the average number of people that a teacher went to for help about a particular topic and gives the reader a sense of the overall amount of advice-seeking connections, per person, in a school. (Mean out-degree was calculated using survey respondent data only.) As measured by mean out-degree, the average teacher went to approximately two people for advice about each of the professional concerns mentioned above: course content and planning, classroom management, and low-performing students. When examining FTF3, for example, we observed that the average teacher went to 1.9 people for advice on course content and planning, 2.1 people for advice on classroom management issues, and 1.9 people for advice about assisting low-performing students. FTF3 was typical of all 15 schools in that the total amount of communication in each of the three professional networks was about the same. We also observed that there was relatively little variation in the total amount of communication among the schools. However, within a given school, there was a lot of variation in the amount of advice sought by individual teachers. In all three networks, over 95% of the variation in out-degree occurred within schools (i.e., among teachers), leaving less than

5% of the variation in total communication to be explained by differences between schools.[3] In sum:

- There was little variation in the total amount of communication across the 15 high schools.
- Within a given school, the amount of communication about course content and planning, classroom management, and low-performing students was about the same.
- The majority of variation in communication occurred at the individual level, where some teachers asked very few or none of their co-workers for advice and others asked many more people for advice.

Isolated Teachers

As Table 4.2 shows, the three professional networks in any given school were also similar with respect to their percentages of isolated teachers. The "isolates" represent those teachers who neither went to anyone for help, nor were sought out for help. Our findings offer supporting evidence for the notion of the isolated teacher (Lortie, 2002). Across all 15 schools, the average percentage of "isolated" teachers in a given network was 31%. That means that nearly one third of all staff surveyed for this study neither sought advice from nor provided advice to colleagues on these three areas of professional concern.

Interestingly, in a given school, the percentage of isolated teachers was relatively consistent across the three topics of conversation. The correlation of the percentage of isolates among our three networks ranged from 0.69 to 0.93. ("Range" refers to the correlations between the "Isolates" columns in Table 4.2.) This range indicates that among the three areas of professional conversation, in most schools one area does not appear to be more "popular" than another for teachers to discuss.

While the percentage of isolated teachers did not vary much across the three professional networks within a school, it did vary considerably among the 15 schools studied. For example, Table 4.2 shows that in FTF1's classroom management network, only 11% of teachers were isolated from their peers, while in RU3's classroom management network 47% of teachers were isolates. In sum:

- On average, nearly one third of all teachers were isolates in any given professional network.
- Within a school, the percentage of isolates was generally similar among the three networks.

Table 4.2. Network descriptive statistics.

		Course Content and Planning		*Classroom Management*		*Low-Performing Students*	
School	*Network Size*	*Mean Out-Degree (number of individuals consulted)*	*Isolates (%)*	*Mean Out-Degree (number of individuals consulted)*	*Isolates (%)*	*Mean Out-Degree (number of individuals consulted)*	*Isolates (%)*
FTF1	159	2.2	18.9	2.7	11.3	2.4	15.1
FTF2	76	1.8	36.8	2.2	34.2	1.6	38.2
FTF3	184	1.9	23.4	2.1	24.5	1.9	19.6
HSTW1	114	2.2	22.8	2.6	26.3	2.0	30.7
HSTW2	114	2.2	24.6	2.7	24.6	2.2	23.7
HSTW3	86	1.1	47.7	1.9	34.9	1.8	33.7
PLN1	123	2.2	32.5	2.5	29.3	2.5	32.5
PLN2	67	1.8	29.9	1.7	20.9	2.4	17.9
PLN3	132	1.8	28.0	2.5	21.2	2.2	25.0
RU1	40	1.3	37.5	2.3	17.5	1.4	20.0
RU2	110	2.2	36.4	2.2	35.5	2.0	30.9
RU3	83	1.8	45.8	2.1	47.0	1.6	54.2
SN1	61	1.1	31.1	1.7	37.7	1.5	31.1
SN2	324	1.7	34.9	2.0	38.0	1.4	43.2
SN3	111	1.9	38.7	1.8	45.0	2.0	46.8
Average	119	1.8	32.6	2.2	29.9	1.9	30.8

Note: Network density was intentionally not included in this table because it is highly correlated (around .70) with network size. Generally, the professional network densities were relatively sparse, ranging from 0.5% to 8% among all 15 schools.

- There was considerable variation across schools in the percentage of staff members who were not engaged in any professional conversation.

Network Modeling

While the communication and isolation data give the impression that our three networks are somewhat redundant, when we examined the patterns of communication, we found that the three networks have distinct characteristics. Using network analysis, we modeled communication to assess the association of a number of variables with the likelihood that one individual will seek advice from another.

Figure 4.2 provides a visual depiction of the network models. In this diagram we see two people who work in one school, person A and person B. The network model predicts the likelihood that person A will go to person B for advice. Whether or not person A goes to person B for advice is the dependent variable in our model, depicted by the arrow between them. We hypothesized that the likelihood that person A would go to person B for advice depended on the individual characteristics of person A and person B, as well as their shared characteristics. For example, we might expect that department chairs are more likely to be sought out for advice about curriculum issues. As a result, we included as an *advice-giver predictor* whether or not person B was a department chair. This enabled us to establish whether department chairs were more likely than non–department chairs to be advice givers. We also might expect that if person A and person B share certain characteristics, for example, if they are both in the same department, this may increase the likelihood that person A will go to person B for advice. Thus, we included several *shared-characteristic predictors.* This enabled us to establish whether the likelihood that person A would go to person B for advice depended on whether or not they were in the same department.

Figure 4.2. The network models.

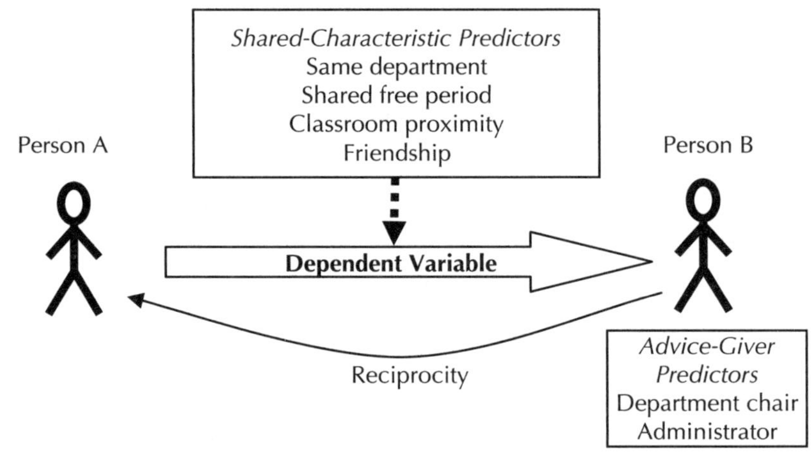

We were particularly interested in a number of variables that are common to many high schools across the United States. Our models included the following predictor variables:

ADVICE-GIVER PREDICTORS

- *Position of department chair or administrator.* We hypothesized that the organization and designation of formal leadership in schools played a role in the construction of communication networks and social capital. The official organization of schools endows certain individuals with leadership credentials through the use of titles and authority over human and physical resources. The hierarchical organization of most high schools (and most institutions of any sort) results in the designation of some people as resources for staff. Administrators (e.g., principals, assistant principals, school improvement facilitators and coordinators, coaches) and academic department chairs stand somewhat apart from the rest of the faculty as a result of their acquisition of an additional title and a slightly different set of responsibilities.
- *Reciprocity.* The reciprocity variable assesses the extent to which an individual being sought out as a source of advice by someone will in turn seek out that person for advice. This variable was included in order to assess the extent to which network ties are reciprocated, as well as to help account for the lack of independence in a network model. Although this variable connects the seeker and the giver of advice, it is included as an advice-giver characteristic because it is based on the likelihood of that person seeking out the other for advice in return.

SHARED-CHARACTERISTIC PREDICTORS

- *Shared membership in the same department.* In high schools, academic departments and other organizational configurations that encourage team-based decision making have been shown to improve communication and collaboration (Supovitz, 2002). The subject-area department, perhaps the most common organizational feature of the American high school, often has been touted as the foundation for professional communication networks (Siskin, 1994; Stodolsky & Grossman, 1995), breaking down teacher isolation.
- *Shared free periods.* If teachers are to begin to communicate about issues of professional concern, they need time for this activity

during the school day. A strategy that has been cited as potentially increasing the social capital in high schools is the creation of common planning times (Louis, Marks, & Kruse, 1996; Warren & Muth, 1995). Sometimes this time is carefully structured by school leaders, while other times it is left open for teachers to use as they see fit. For this reason, we included the presence of a shared preparation or lunch period among the possible predictor variables.

- *Shared physical location (classroom proximity)*. Physical proximity also has been shown to foster the type of relationships that contribute to social networks. "Employees tend to develop informal relationships with others who work close to them" (Brass, 1985, p. 329). And since "the more frequently persons interact with one another, the stronger their sentiments of friendship for one another are apt to be" (Homans, 1950, p. 133), it is likely that individuals working in proximity to one another will become friends. Because people who are friends are likely to discuss professional issues (Frank, Zhao, & Borman, 2004), we hypothesized that classroom proximity in schools will lead to developing professional relationships.
- *Friendship*. Research has shown that when two people have a social connection, they are more likely to turn to each other for advice and to adopt each other's practices (Degenne & Forse, 1999; Weinbaum, Supovitz, Gross, Cole, Weiss, & Ricalde, 2006). In the qualitative data that were collected as part of this study, interview respondents corroborated this finding, often indicating that their friends were frequent sources of advice. For this reason, we included friendship connections as one of the predictor variables. Information about friendship connections among individuals was collected as part of the survey questions identified earlier (see Table 4.1).

Our general findings from this analysis can be summed up as follows: Department chairs and administrators across all three professional networks were more likely to be the recipients of requests for advice than nondepartment chairs and nonadministrators. Additionally, staff tended to seek professional advice from people who were in their same department, whose classrooms were in close proximity, and with whom they were friends. Sharing a free period was not associated with advice-seeking behavior.

While these general results held true across the three professional networks, the relative strength of the predictor variables depended on the area in which advice was sought. A comparison of the beta coefficients in Table 4.3 illustrates the relative strength of each independent variable in predicting the likelihood of communication in a given network. For example, when seeking advice about course content and planning, the strongest predictor of communication was whether or not the advice seeker and giver belonged to the same department. The fact that belonging to the same department was very important to those seeking advice on course content and planning is not surprising since, for high school teachers, course content is often specialized information about which people outside the department are less likely to be knowledgeable. Qualitative data gathered as part of this study confirmed the result, with many teachers reporting that when looking for advice about what to cover in class, they sought out colleagues who were teaching or had taught the same course.

In contrast, when teachers were seeking advice about classroom management, the strongest predictor variable was whether or not the receiver was an administrator. This result confirms the popular notion that teachers tend to go to their principal or assistant principal to discuss discipline issues. Much of the authority and ability to sanction problematic student behavior is granted to the formal leadership of the school, and therefore administrators are clear sources of support for teachers regarding classroom management.

Finally, when teachers were seeking advice about assisting low-performing students, the most powerful predictor of communication was whether or not two individuals were friends. This indicates that when seeking advice on helping struggling students, teachers sought out people whom they trusted. When faced with underperforming students, teachers had to reveal a certain limitation in their knowledge and ability to address student needs. It is logical that this would be done most easily with colleagues with whom they had a friendship connection and a tradition of sharing personal issues. In sum:

- Across all three professional networks, teachers tended to seek advice from staff in their same department, administrators, friends, department chairs, and staff whose classrooms were nearby.
- In seeking advice about course content and planning, the strongest predictor of a relationship was whether or not two staff members were in the same department.
- In seeking advice about classroom management, the strongest predictor of a relationship was whether or not the advice giver was an administrator.
- In seeking advice about assisting low-performing students, the strongest predictor of a relationship was whether or not two staff members were friends.

Table 4.3. Variables related to communication in the professional networks.

Network	Predictor Variable	Standardized Estimate	Standardized Coefficient Standard Error	Raw Estimate Odds Ratio
Course content and planning	Intercept	−5.7***	(0.1)	0.00
	Reciprocity	74.8***	(3.6)	6.05
	Department Chair (receiver)	132.8***	(12.0)	4.18
	Administrator (receiver)	157.5***	(12.9)	6.75
	Same Department	291.6***	(7.2)	13.87
	Shared Free Period	17.4	(12.4)	1.09
	Proximity	94.0***	(6.5)	2.86
	Friendship	136.2***	(3.9)	11.70
Classroom management	Intercept	−5.4***	(0.1)	0.00
	Reciprocity	43.8***	(3.8)	2.94
	Department Chair (receiver)	113.3***	(12.6)	3.39
	Administrator (receiver)	252.3***	(11.5)	21.33
	Same Department	178.1***	(7.3)	5.00
	Shared Free Period	30.6*	(12.4)	1.17
	Proximity	91.6***	(6.5)	2.77
	Friendship	176.6***	(3.7)	24.29
Low-performing students	Intercept	−5.2***	(0.1)	0.00
	Reciprocity	43.1***	(4.0)	3.00
	Department Chair (receiver)	68.6***	(15.0)	2.10
	Administrator (receiver)	148.3***	(14.3)	6.05
	Same Department	138.1***	(7.6)	3.49
	Shared Free Period	−1.7	(12.4)	0.99
	Proximity	72.3***	(6.9)	2.23
	Friendship	160.7***	(3.8)	18.17

Note: $N = 161{,}207$.
$^{*}p < .05$. $^{***}p < .001$.

In combination, these findings point to some very significant impacts of traditional structures and characteristics on professional communication in high schools. Sharing departmental membership or friendship ties, or being a department chair or other administrator, consistently showed the strongest ability to predict communication ties. Variables such as physical proximity and reciprocity also proved to be significant predictors, but to a lesser extent. Free periods, as a shared characteristic, proved to be insignificant after accounting for the other factors. These findings tell us a lot about the factors associated with communication in the traditional high school organization.

The analysis described above included 14 high schools[4] and considered them as if they were typical high schools. However, as we know, the high schools in this study had partnered with external school reform organizations that brought particular strategies (structural and nonstructural) of their own. In the next section, we look at the reform programs and how they related to high school communication patterns.

HOW THE REFORM PROGRAMS ARE RELATED TO IN-SCHOOL COMMUNICATION

The reforms in this study could have influenced school communication patterns in two potential ways: (1) through structural or organizational changes that were introduced to enhance professional development and planning, and (2) by providing training directly to individuals, without structural changes. We sought to better understand the influences that these two approaches to reform had on communication, under the premise that communication would be related to the knowledge, experiences, values, and norms that impact changes in teacher practice. Later in this chapter we will discuss the relationship between communication patterns and changes in staff attitude and behavior related to reform. It will become apparent that the relationship between communication and attitude should be of certain concern to those interested in reform.

In this study, two of the five reforms studied, First Things First (FTF) and High Schools That Work (HSTW), make explicit use of new organizational structures to catalyze patterns of communication in order to improve teacher practice and student achievement. Structural changes, such as the creation of multigrade interdisciplinary teacher teams and the development of staff planning and improvement teams, are implemented in schools to stimulate communication among staff members.

Two other reforms, Penn Literacy Network (PLN) and SchoolNet (SN), attempt to make use of preexisting communication patterns in high schools to spread their practices. They provide training directly to teachers and staff without requiring any particular organizational changes. The final reform, Ramp-Up to Literacy (RU), generally does not view spread of the reform as a primary goal and thus has relatively little use for the concept of social networks. Given this difference in the ways the reforms view social networks, we focused our analysis heavily on the two reforms (FTF and HSTW) that attempt to make explicit use of new school structures in their reform efforts.

Professional Communication and Structural or Organizational Changes

As discussed in earlier chapters, a central component of FTF is the creation of small learning communities (SLCs). The main objective of creating SLCs is the formation of closer relationships among students, school staff, and families. For most schools, the creation of SLCs shifts the organizational structure from one that centers on the academic department to one where groupings are interdepartmental. FTF's theory of action expects that creating SLCs, and setting aside specific time for staff to meet with their SLC team members, will lead to changes in communication patterns within the school. We found that this structural change did in fact lead to patterns of staff communication that were more centered within the SLCs.

Social network analysis was employed to examine the communication patterns in the schools that had partnered with FTF. Of particular interest was whether or not the shared characteristic of belonging to the same SLC was associated with an increased likelihood of communication among school staff. It was expected that as schools were further along in implementing FTF, belonging to the same SLC would be a significant predictor of communication.

Our study included three schools implementing FTF. At the time of our first survey, FTF1 had recently created SLCs, FTF2 had fully functioning SLCs in place for 1 year, and FTF3 had been structured around SLCs for 5 years. In FTF1, staff had been assigned to SLCs, but the SLCs had yet to meet regularly at the time of data collection. As a result, in FTF1 we did *not* expect that teachers who belonged to the same SLC would be any more likely to seek one another out for advice than teachers who belonged to different SLCs.

The social network data confirmed our hypotheses. Figure 4.3 plots the magnitude of the same SLC predictor for each of the three schools in each of the three communication networks (course content and planning, classroom management, and strategies for assisting low-performing students). The larger the value of the "same SLC" coefficient, the greater the likelihood of one person seeking out another for advice when those two people belong to the same SLC compared with when the two people belong to different SLCs. In FTF1, we found that belonging to the same

Figure 4.3. Magnitude of same SLC coefficient in modeling network communication.

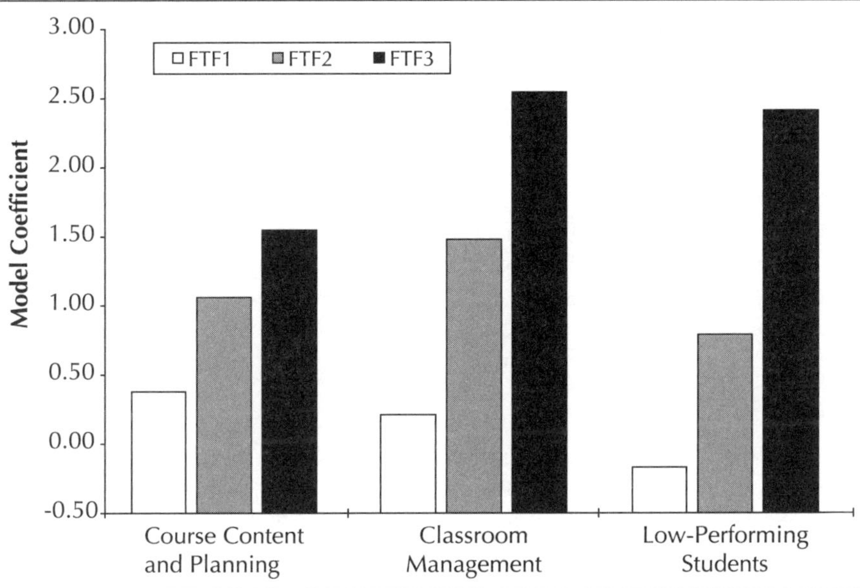

Note: The parameter estimates for FTF1 are not significantly different from zero.

SLC was *not* a statistically significant predictor of communication in the three professional networks. In FTF2 and FTF3, if two people belonged to the same SLC, this significantly increased the likelihood that one would go to the other for advice about a host of professional concerns.

As evidenced by looking at the set of bars for each network, in the schools that were further along in their implementation of FTF, belonging to the same SLC had a stronger association with the likelihood that a staff member would go to another staff member for advice. This trend provides supporting evidence for the idea that as schools move along in the implementation of FTF, school staff increasingly go to people within their SLC for advice. Although the trend in the data is consistent, no causal conclusions can be drawn.

A similar, but weaker, pattern was seen in the three HSTW schools in the study. For the purpose of this structural analysis, HSTW's primary organizational change—the creation of focus teams—was considered analogous to the SLCs in FTF. In HSTW1, which was in its first year of focus team organization, we observed that teachers who shared a focus team were more likely to go to one another for advice in one professional network only: strategies for assisting low-performing students. In HSTW2, which had had focus teams for a couple of years, if two people belonged to the same focus team, this significantly increased the likelihood that one would go to the other for advice about course content and planning as well as for strategies for assisting low-performing students. Although HSTW3 had implemented HSTW for the longest period of time, we saw very little influence of the focus teams in this school. This was likely because just prior to our survey this school's five focus teams had been reorganized into three larger teams. The reshuffling of staff into the new, larger focus teams, some with new chairpeople, made this school more like a first-year implementer of focus teams. For this reason, the patterns of communication in our sample of HSTW schools did not hold as clearly as with FTF, but the analysis still provides some supporting evidence that structural changes can impact communication patterns. In sum:

- We found evidence in support of the claim that structural changes can impact communication patterns within a school, but we did not find any evidence that the total *amount* of communication is any different as a result of these organizational changes.
- The likelihood that one staff member would go to another staff member for advice increased significantly if the two staff members belonged to the same organizational structure (i.e., SLCs or focus teams).

Professional Communication and Training

In contrast to the reforms with restructuring components, three of the reforms examined—RU, PLN, and SN—did not require explicit strategies for altering patterns of communication within the school. In addition, while *all* staff members in FTF and HSTW were impacted by the reforms through both the restructuring of the school and professional development training about the reform, this was not necessarily the case in the nonstructural reforms. In the RU, PLN, and SN reforms, professional development was not provided to all school staff.

Although no formal strategy exists for spreading the RU, PLN, and SN reforms as part of their designs, we hypothesized that school staff with professional development training in the reform might become natural resources for other staff about certain professional practices. These reforms all seek to improve achievement of low-performing students, so this would be the most logical network in which to see a potential impact. To test this hypothesis, we examined whether staff who had been trained in the practices of the reform were more likely than staff without professional training to be the recipients of requests for advice in any of the three professional networks. The evidence from the network analysis did not demonstrate that professional training played a role in advice-seeking activity around traditional professional practice. We found that staff members with reform-specific professional development training were no more likely to receive requests for advice about traditional professional concerns than staff without this training. In these cases, perhaps because the majority of our evidence came from schools that were still relatively early in the implementation process, we did not find the same kinds of impact on communication that we found in the reforms with structural modifications.

THE PROVIDER NETWORK AS A DEPENDENT VARIABLE

As shown in the previous section, the presence of certain reforms was associated with particular patterns of communication in the traditional areas of professional communication. However, the introduction of a reform also precipitated the creation of a new communication network. That is the network we labeled "provider network" and it includes the individuals who seek out others for advice about the reform in their school.

In addition to typical conversations regarding professional concerns (described in the previous sections), teachers in the study schools also discussed the reform being implemented. The nature of this communication was very different from the three professional networks, both in terms of the amount of communication and how this communication was distributed throughout the schools. This section discusses the communication about the reform (the provider network).

Sparseness of the Provider Network

Teachers generally did not turn to one another for advice regarding the reform as often as they did for advice about other professional issues analyzed in this study. The average teacher respondent sought out less than one other person for advice about the reform in his or her school (average out-degree across the 15 schools was 0.83).[5] There was variability in the amount of conversation across schools: Average requests for help ranged from a low of 0.25 in PLN1 to a high of 1.47 in FTF2.

As can be seen in Table 4.4, provider networks related to the two whole-school reforms had much more conversation than those related to the three more targeted reforms. The mean out-degree for FTF and HSTW

Table 4.4. Provider network descriptive statistics.

		Provider	
School	*Network Size*	*Mean Out-Degree (number of individuals consulted)*	*Isolates (%)*
FTF1	159	1.1	44.7
FTF2	76	1.5	46.1
FTF3	184	1.0	46.2
HSTW1	114	1.5	36.8
HSTW2	114	1.3	44.7
HSTW3	86	1.3	39.5
PLN1	123	0.2	90.2
PLN2	67	0.4	86.6
PLN3	132	1.1	53.8
RU1	40	0.3	82.5
RU2	110	0.7	80.9
RU3	83	0.6	80.7
SN1	61	0.7	60.7
SN2	324	0.4	79.3
SN3	111	0.3	82.0
Average	119	0.8	63.6

schools was 1.27, whereas the mean out-degree for RU, PLN, and SN was only 0.53. Not only did schools using the whole-school reforms have more requests for assistance, they also had much lower percentages of isolates (those staff members who neither sought out nor were sought out for advice). Between 37% and 46% of teachers were isolated in the whole-school reforms, while teacher isolates ranged from 54% to 90% in the other three reforms.[6] This level of teacher isolation may be a better indicator of the spread (or lack thereof) of communication in the schools than the average number of requests for help.

These results are logical given the details of the reform designs. As discussed in the previous section, FTF and HSTW are whole-school reforms intended to reach all teachers.[7] These models provide professional training to all teachers and restructure the groupings of teachers within the school, strategies that impact all teachers in a school. In contrast, the RU, PLN, and SN designs do not call for restructuring the school and provide targeted training to some, but not all, teachers. These reforms do not build into their designs a strategy for reaching all school staff. Table 4.4 shows the differential impact of these strategies on the amount of communication about the reform. In sum:

- There was less conversation about the reform than about traditional professional practice.
- The majority of individuals in schools implementing the more targeted reforms (RU, PLN, and SN) were not involved in communication about the reform at all.

Modeling the Provider Network

Having established the relative lack of communication in the provider network in comparison with the professional networks, we were curious to know whether the provider network was influenced by similar individual and shared organizational characteristics. Using the same analysis process described earlier, we estimated the organizational characteristics that predict advice seeking in the provider network. As we saw in the professional networks, department chairs and administrators were more likely than people not in those roles to receive requests for provider-related advice. Furthermore, as before, being in the same department and having classrooms in close physical proximity were associated with an increased likelihood of advice-seeking activity. In the provider network, the strongest predictors of advice-seeking behaviors were a previous friendship connection between the two people and whether or not the person being sought out for advice was an administrator. Table 4.5 provides estimates for the impact of each variable in the provider network. The reader will note that the relationship between communication and the variables listed is not terribly different from the relationship reported for traditional areas of professional communication.

These aggregated results were estimated by combining all schools in the sample together in one model. However, this strategy ignores the unique changes that reforms bring to schools in terms of both structure and training, as discussed previously. Accordingly, the predictors of communication about the reform programs will be investigated in greater depth, taking into account the reform strategies. In sum:

- The influence of predictor variables in the provider network follows a pattern similar to that established in the networks for course content and planning, classroom management, and low-performing students.

Table 4.5. Variables related to communication in the provider network.

Predictor Variable	*Standardized Estimate*	*Standardized Coefficient Standard Error*	*Raw Estimate Odds Ratio*
Intercept	–6.45***	0.19	–6.84
Reciprocity	32.75***	4.63	1.25
Department Chair (receiver)	75.97***	18.95	0.82
Administrator (receiver)	152.75***	17.98	1.85
Same Department	130.10***	11.61	1.17
Shared Free Period	35.69	18.76	0.19
Proximity	74.96***	10.05	0.84
Friendship	145.48***	5.72	2.62

Note: $N = 161{,}207$.
*** $p < .001$.

- Examining communication about all of the reforms as a single group overlooks important differences in the strategies that the reforms introduced to the schools.

Visibility of Reform Effects in the Provider Network

Earlier, we demonstrated that the presence of SLCs and focus teams was a significant predictor of communication in some professional networks. However, merely attending professional development training in RU, PLN, or SN strategies did not result in a greater likelihood of being a source of advice about traditional professional concerns. Thus, it appeared that structural changes were more influential on teacher communication patterns than was the provision of teacher training.

However, this same finding was not true when we looked at the effects of the reform on the provider network itself. The reform, whether structural or nonstructural, exhibited effects most strongly in communication about the reform. Whether the reform promoted structural change or provided only professional development to teachers, both of these strategies were associated with changes in communication about the reform.

Teachers in schools using FTF tended to request help in the provider network from those teachers in the same SLCs and from SLC coordinators. As we saw in the previous section, shared SLC membership became important in many areas of professional conversation. Interestingly, but perhaps not surprisingly, it was *most* important in predicting conversation around FTF itself.

The HSTW restructuring of schools had a similar effect on the provider network. Individuals who were on the same focus team were more likely to communicate with one another than were individuals who were on different focus teams. However, unlike in FTF, this shared membership was not the strongest predictor of conversation about the reform. In the two more mature schools (HSTW2 and HSTW3), the strongest predictor of conversation about the reform was whether or not the person being sought out for advice was a focus team chair. Unlike in the traditional professional networks, here both focus team membership and being a focus team chair were associated with communication about the reform.

The other three reforms rely on professional development in order to change the practice of teachers. In the professional networks, it was noted that those teachers who had received training were not significantly more likely to be seen as a source of information. However, in the provider network, those teachers who had received training *were* more likely to be sought out for information. Table 4.6 illustrates this point for PLN; see also

Table 4.6. PLN selection model provider network.

	Typical School Variables			*Including Reform Variable*		
Effect	*Standardized Estimate*	*Standardized Coefficient Standard Error*	*Odds Ratio*	*Standardized Estimate*	*Standardized Coefficient Standard Error*	*Odds Ratio*
Intercept	–6.6***	(0.3)	0.00	–6.9***	(0.2)	0.00
Reciprocity	30.1***	(3.9)	18.92	24.9***	(3.9)	11.36
Department Chair (receiver)	67.1***	(14.8)	8.85	58.5***	(15.1)	6.69
Same Department	29.2*	(11.2)	2.05	27.7*	(11.1)	1.97
Shared Free Period	–14.9	(17.1)	0.82	–27.7	(17.1)	0.69
Proximity	26.3*	(10.8)	1.95	25.0*	(10.8)	1.90
Friendship	58.3***	(6.9)	10.07	60.4***	(7.0)	10.90
Trainee (receiver)				128.8***	(21.4)	7.92

Notes: $N = 22{,}008$. The Administrator variable was omitted from this model because in the provider network, no requests for advice were directed at administrators.

* $p < .05$. *** $p < .001$.

Tables 4.7 and 4.8 for similar information for RU and SN, respectively. In the case of PLN, using only the traditional high school variables to explain the provider network leaves one with the impression that as a receiver of requests for advice, being a department chair was the single biggest predictor of the likelihood of a communication link. However, when we included reform-specific strategies—in the case of PLN, the fact that some portion of the faculty had taken a particular course—we saw that the biggest predictor of communication about the reform was whether the receiver of requests for advice had been *trained in the reform*. The same was true for RU, as can be seen in Table 4.7.

Overall, these findings demonstrate the importance of every reform effort in influencing communication around the reform itself. Although we illustrated earlier that structural reforms are associated with changes in communication in many areas of professional concern, here we see that training (without structural change) also can be highly associated with changes in school communication, even though its effects may be more limited in scope. In sum:

Table 4.7. RU selection model provider network.

	Typical School Variables			*Including Reform Variable*		
Effect	*Standardized Estimate*	*Standardized Coefficient Standard Error*	*Odds Ratio*	*Standardized Estimate*	*Standardized Coefficient Standard Error*	*Odds Ratio*
Intercept	–6.5***	(0.3)	0.00	–6.8***	(0.3)	0.00
Reciprocity	0.7	(5.0)	1.11	–3.8	(5.0)	0.58
Department Chair (receiver)	8.1	(17.6)	1.39	–7.6	(19.1)	0.73
Administrator (receiver)	18.0	(19.2)	1.86	30.6	(19.2)	2.86
Same Department	39.0***	(10.1)	4.31	36.1***	(10.2)	3.90
Shared Free Period	8.3	(18.0)	1.19	–4.2	(18.4)	0.91
Adjacent	–5.1	(12.2)	0.84	–9.2	(12.4)	0.73
Friendship	39.5***	(7.3)	7.85	41.6***	(7.5)	8.76
Trainee (receiver)				79.9***	(16.9)	9.30

Note: $N = 11{,}035$.

*** $p < .001$.

Table 4.8. SN selection model provider network.

	Typical School Variables			*Including Reform Variable*		
Effect	*Standardized Estimate*	*Standardized Coefficient Standard Error*	*Odds Ratio*	*Standardized Estimate*	*Standardized Coefficient Standard Error*	*Odds Ratio*
Intercept	–7.3***	(0.5)	0.00	–7.3***	(0.5)	0.00
Reciprocity	–1.9	(7.7)	0.79	–2.6	(7.6)	0.73
Department Chair (receiver)	63.7*	(25.7)	3.13	61.0*	(26.1)	2.97
Administrator (receiver)	62.1*	(27.2)	5.16	68.4*	(27.6)	6.11
Same Department	87.0***	(19.5)	3.46	85.6***	(19.5)	3.39
Shared Free Period	20.3	(28.6)	1.19	19.2	(28.6)	1.17
Adjacent	43.2***	(14.4)	2.61	42.7***	(14.5)	2.59
Friendship	74.7***	(7.7)	17.81	74.5***	(7.7)	17.81
Trainee (receiver)				59.3	(36.7)	1.70

Notes: $N = 62{,}128$. In this model, Trainee = 1 if receiver attended more than one session.
* $p < .05$. *** $p < .001$.

- The whole-school reforms were associated with provider networks that connected greater proportions of school staff members than were the more targeted reforms.
- The effects of the reform programs are strongest, and in fact play a significantly influential role, on communication about the reform itself.

THE RELATIONSHIP BETWEEN ESTABLISHED NETWORKS AND THE PROVIDER NETWORK

As indicated earlier, the network of communication about the reform (the provider network) was less dense and had a much greater proportion of isolated individuals than the other networks of professional communication. Furthermore, the provider network was the area of communication where both the reform structures and trainings were most influential in predicting conversation. Because the provider network appeared very different from the more traditional modes of conversation in these schools, one might consider this network to be an atypical communication pattern. However, it will be shown that in certain contexts, conversation about the reform grew over time and became more similar to existing school communication patterns.

A second round of data collection allowed us to examine the changes in communication over time. This second round of data included 644 surveys, with response rates ranging from 55% to 89% (average response rate was 77%). The round two survey sampled nine of the early-implementing schools instead of the entire sample of 10 schools because of the closing of FTF2 (mentioned earlier). The results in this section and the following one draw on comparisons of these nine schools over the two periods; the decreased sample size is not a threat to the validity of the reported results.

In this section, we draw on both the first and second rounds of survey data and show that communication about the reform is the most dynamic and evolving communication network in the schools, relative to traditional professional communication. Furthermore, as the provider network "grows," it becomes increasingly similar to the schools' other conversation patterns. This evidence is particularly compelling because we are looking at schools that were completing only their second or third year of work with the reform at the time of the second survey.

Growth of the Provider Network over Time

Over time, an increased number of individuals became involved in conversation about the reform. Not only did individuals report seeking advice from more people about the reform, but a smaller percentage of staff members were isolated or disconnected from the provider network. Ultimately, the proportion of isolated individuals in the provider network decreased in six of the nine schools. These results speak to a growing level of communication around the reform. The reform gained ground through conversation, and thus information about the reform became more accessible to more staff members.

The "growth" of the provider network is especially compelling when it is considered relative to the three professional networks. In general, the total amount of communication *decreased* over time in the professional networks. In only two of the nine schools was there an increase in the number of individuals talking about course content and planning, and in only one school was there an increased amount of conversation about low-performing students.[8] These results are indicated in Table 4.9, where the differences in average out-degree (number of requests for help) are displayed for each school. The number of requests for help about the reform increased in four schools, which is considerable relative to the decreases noted in the professional networks. Additionally, in those schools where there were fewer requests for help about the reform in the second year, the decrease was smaller than in any of the other networks. In contrast to the diminishing nature of the professional networks, we can see that communication about the reform was growing, or at the very least showed less decay.

The Increasing Integration of the Provider Network in the School over Time

Not only did the provider networks increase in size and encompass greater percentages of staff over time, but these networks became more similar to conversation paths about other areas of practice. The established professional communication pathways were used increasingly as avenues for requests for help about the reform. Stated another way, "overlap" of the provider network onto traditional professional conversation increased between the two data collection points.

Teachers increasingly tended to talk about the reform with those whom they sought out for advice about other professional concerns. Although the amounts of the increases in overlap between the provider network and other networks in any given school were relatively small,

Table 4.9. Change in average requests for advice per survey respondent from 2005 to 2006.

School	*ClassMgmt*	*Content/Plan*	*LowPerf*	*Provider*
RU1	–0.60	0.07	0.43	0.50
RU2	–0.53	–0.93	–0.82	0.15
SN1	–0.26	–0.23	–0.60	–0.13
SN2	–0.50	–0.30	–0.29	0.00
FTF1	–0.62	–0.38	–0.59	0.03
HSTW1	–0.45	–0.70	–0.44	0.21
HSTW2	–0.50	–0.64	–0.78	–0.37
PLN1	–0.67	–0.58	–1.15	–0.13
PLN2	–0.04	0.10	–0.48	–0.04

there was at least some increase in network overlap in 59% of the pairings between provider network and any of the other networks.[9] In RU1, for example, only 4% of provider conversations overlapped with discipline conversations at the first data collection point; by the second data collection point this increased to 21%. The provider network appears to have become most integrated with the low-performing students network, as increases in network overlap between the provider and low-performing students networks occurred in seven of the nine schools. This finding is interesting because of the ambition of some of the reforms to particularly target those students most in need of overcoming performance challenges. We do not want to overstate the degree to which the provider network increasingly overlapped with networks of more traditional professional communication in these schools: In 25% of the cases, the change in network overlap was negative. This indicates that in these cases the provider network became even more different than other networks in the schools.

Overall, the provider network tended to increasingly overlap with the existing communication patterns of the school over time, as evidenced by the relative increase in communication about the reform and the increasing overlap of reform conversation with traditional professional communication. This suggests that communication about the reforms and communication about other areas of professional concern in the school needed time in order to become more alike.

The network relationships described above may be summarized as follows:

- The provider network exhibited greater growth than the other three professional networks. Over time, there was less teacher isolation and increased overall conversation regarding the reform.
- The provider network displayed greater overlap with the three professional networks over time and therefore became increasingly part of the school culture.

THE EFFECT OF IN-SCHOOL COMMUNICATION ON ATTITUDES AND BEHAVIORS ABOUT THE REFORM

In the previous sections, we demonstrated that certain reform strategies can impact existing communication patterns. Furthermore, the introduction of a reform in a school resulted in a new communication pattern particular to the reform, and this structure grew over time to become increasingly incorporated into existing school culture. In this section, we will argue that there are characteristics of an organization that facilitate conversation about the reform, and that the amount of communication about the reform is correlated with attitudes and behaviors related to the reform.

The Relationship Between Professional Network Size and Provider Network Growth

Having established in the previous section that communication about the reform tended to grow (relative to other professional communication) between the two rounds of data collection, we looked at the conditions under which communication about the reform was more or less likely to increase. Our data show that schools with initially more sparse professional networks were associated with relatively large growth in the amount of communication in the provider network. Similarly, more dense professional networks at the first data collection point were associated with low (or negative) growth in the provider network density. From these results, it becomes clear that the change in the amount of communication about the reform was not uniform across all schools, and perhaps was impacted by the amount of professional communication at the first data collection point.

These results may speak to the ability of a school to take on a reform and incorporate it into the school culture. In schools where there were low levels of professional conversation, it appears that staff were more successful in building a more robust communication network about the new reform. As we established at the outset, school staff members create communication networks, and the introduction of a reform in schools where communication is limited creates an opportunity, or "space," for reform to be embraced as a growing component of school conversation.

An alternative view of this relationship is that in schools where a rich collaborative environment exists around areas of traditional professional concern, it may be more difficult for reform to take hold and become part of the school culture. If the individuals in the school are already involved in deep professional dialogues, they may reject a new reform or practice in order to maintain the status quo of the organization, or they may not feel the need to seek advice from others about the reform. In organizations where extensive professional collaboration occurs, individuals may have a positive opinion of the current status of the school, and therefore will be less inclined to incorporate the reform into their conversations.

Changes in Attitudes and Behaviors as Well as Communication Patterns

The negative correlation between the total initial amount of professional communication and the change in provider network communication demonstrates that reform conversation tended to grow in schools with sparse professional networks. However, an increase in provider-related communication is not the single desired impact that a reform attempts to bring to a school. Rather, these five providers entered schools with the hope that their reforms would alter the behaviors of the teachers and administrators in order to improve student performance. Thus, the goals of providers are to have the school staff both modify their classroom practices and engage in conversation.

In the survey, a series of questions was asked regarding attitudes about the reform, as well as questions pertaining to use of particular strategies related to each reform. Two scale scores were developed from these questions to account for (1) individual attitude regarding the reform, and (2) the frequency with which each provider's strategies were used in individual classroom practice. The changes in these attitude and implementation scale scores are, therefore, outcomes of interest in measuring the impact of the reform in obtaining/achieving its true goals.

The Association Between Changes in Communication and Changes in Attitude

In examining the relationship between network connections and attitude about the reform, we found that teachers who engaged in more conversation over time about the reform were the ones whose attitudes toward the reform also improved over that same time period.[10]

While this positive relationship between provider network communication and attitude about the reform generally existed across the nine schools, there were two schools where this relationship did not hold. In these two schools there was a negative correlation between the change in individual attitude and the size of the provider ego-network. In FTF1, average individual attitudes toward the reform declined over time, in spite of an increase in the average size of the provider network within the school. The second survey came at the end of this school's first year of work with FTF and shows the spread of the reform to reach more people, some of whom initially may have been resistant. Conversely, in PLN1, average individual attitudes actually improved, in spite of decreasing average size in individual provider ego-networks. This school had ended its partnership with PLN by the time of the second survey so it is not surprising that the provider network shrank. It is interesting to note that teachers continued to feel positively disposed toward the reform. Therefore, the positive relationship between provider network size and attitude toward the reform did not occur in all of the schools surveyed, the original regression results notwithstanding.

While most schools demonstrated an improvement in attitudes over time, accompanied by an increase in provider network size, two schools (PLN2 and SN2) exhibited a decline in individual attitudes along with a decrease in provider network size. The fact that the trend of the relationship between the two variables is in the expected direction supports an association between network growth and improvement in attitude. While a causal relationship between provider network size and attitude toward the reform cannot be elicited from these data, there is ample evidence to suggest that there may be a viable association between these variables.[11]

These results echo the results of Coleman (1986) and Turner (1988) that individual sentiments are affected by interactions. Other research has shown that attitude formation and change occur primarily through social interactions (Erickson, 1988). Similarly, research has demonstrated that teacher influences on one another must be accounted for when designing or implementing a strategy to change teacher sentiments or behaviors (Darling-Hammond & McLaughlin, 1995; Zeichner & Gore, 1989). Our data support the contention that the growth of communication about a particular topic, an external school reform in this case, can and does relate to teacher attitudes and beliefs.

The Association Between Changes in Communication and Changes in Behavior

A second set of analyses was performed to examine the relationship between changes in communication networks and teacher behavior regarding use of particular practices encouraged by the reform. Since each of the five providers focused on different aspects of change in teacher practice, different survey behavior questions were necessary for the five different reforms. Consequently, the scales for each of these implementation scores were not combined into a single regression, as was done to assess relationships to attitudes. Instead, correlations were performed on individual provider network size and individual implementation scores in order to characterize this relationship.

The results using the implementation scores reflect the same relationship that was noted using the attitude scale: Teachers whose provider networks grew over time were also the same teachers who reported using practices supported by the reform. Although the results for the relationship between network size and implementation were not as strong as those for attitude change, it is encouraging that those who were more connected to conversation about the reform also tended to report that they were using the practices supported by the reform. In seven out of the eight schools,[12] there was a positive correlation between change in provider ego-network size and change in implementation. Only in PLN1 was there a negative correlation between these two variables. Looking across the schools, the small size of change in behavior is not terribly surprising given the brief period of time between survey administrations. Additionally, because some schools were completing their third year of implementation at the time of our second survey, the types of basic practices that can be captured on a survey likely were already present in many of the target classrooms at the time of our first data collection.

How in-school communication affects reform attitudes and behavior may be summarized as follows:

- Schools with relatively sparse professional networks had relatively large growth in their provider networks.
- Individuals who were more involved in conversations about the reform had the greatest change in their attitudes and behaviors regarding the reform.

Conclusion

In the sections above, we have answered each of the research questions stated at the outset and in doing so made a case for the importance of studying communication patterns in high schools. Reviewing this chapter, we see that staff members' connectedness to a communication network was related to their positive attitudes and behaviors in support of the reform. Although this work is not able to document a clear causal relationship, it does point to a quantifiable relationship between school communication and reform practice. In this chapter we also demonstrated that these important communication networks related to reform are most likely to grow in schools where professional conversations are relatively sparse and sporadic. Although some research suggests that reforms are easiest to make in schools that have developed professional communities, our finding would suggest that we might expect, at least in the short term, the greatest activity around a reform to occur in those schools with relatively limited professional communication. Given these findings, it is clear that both schools and providers must consider carefully the existing conditions before formulating expectations for progress and attempting to introduce reform. Furthermore, once the reform has been introduced, schools must facilitate and promote conversations about the reform in order to increase the likelihood that it will yield intended outcomes.

Our findings also suggest ways in which communication links are forged in high schools. We found that staff members regularly view school administrators and department chairs as resources for advice. Additionally, the traditional academic department structure remains highly associated with teacher communication, with teachers turning to their department peers for advice. All of this points to the association between organizational structures and staff communication. This association is further supported by the finding that clear organizational structures introduced by a reform were associated with changes in communication for schools with varying years of experience with the reform. Although training particular individuals in reform practices was associated with those people attracting disproportionate requests for advice about the reform itself, they did not become resources in other areas of professional concern. This contrasts with the relationship between endowing an individual with a formal title and responsibility, which was associated with increased requests for advice across a number of professional domains (even when the title or responsibility was specifically related to the reform).

Overall, our evidence points to the persistence of traditional structures in influencing communication patterns in high schools, even when new practices are introduced. The persistence of communication patterns reinforces the persistence that we see in practice and the difficulty that reforms have in making changes in practice. We do not argue that changes in practice follow closely or uniformly on the heels of changes in communication, although we clearly see a relationship. And in contrast to some perceptions of high schools, our research shows that communication networks are not impervious to reform; changes to communication come relatively quickly and broadly when reform is accompanied by structural change. Changes in communication appear to be more narrowly focused (at least during the first few years) when reform is pursued through training without structural change.

This chapter also aims to provide researchers and practitioners with a glimpse of what can be done using social network analysis in planning for and executing school reform efforts. Insights into who is sought out for advice (to be discussed in more depth in Chapter 5), who is isolated from professional communication, what structures and opportunities impact communication, and the impact that communication exerts on a reform are all tools that could serve well in our ongoing effort to improve educational opportunities at the high school level.

NOTES

1. As described in Chapter 1 and the Appendix, surveys were conducted at all schools in the spring of 2005 and again at nine early-implementing schools in the spring of 2006. The majority of the discussion in this chapter is based on the first round of survey data collected. This included 1,052 teacher surveys. School response rates ranged from 57% to 89%, with an average response rate of 75%.

2. Limiting the potential responses to five colleagues may have impacted the data collected. However, few of our respondents provided up to five names, suggesting that the limit did not constrain the potential information. Only 15% of respondents provided either four or five names.

3. Variance partitioning was calculated using a random effects ANOVA with no fixed effects predictors

4. The network models used 14 schools (rather than all 15 schools that were in the study) because data collection opportunities at FTF2 were curtailed due to a natural disaster. Without a full set of data for that school, it could not be effectively included in the models.

5. Average out-degree scores for the course content, classroom management, and low-performing students networks were 1.8, 2.2, and 1.9, respectively.

6. It is possible that in two of the targeted reforms (RU and PLN) conversations were focused within the English departments, and as a result, aggregated school-level results may not be appropriate. These descriptive statistics were included to illustrate the differences in provider-related communication across reforms.

7. PLN3, where PLN was implemented as a whole-school reform, has results more like the two whole-school reforms (see Table 4.4).

8. The overwhelming majority of average out-degree scores decreased from the first round to the second round of data collection in the traditional professional networks in all schools. While this may have been due to a true decline in conversation, it is also possible that it was due to a modification in the survey, whereby respondents were asked to fill in a circle if they did not seek advice from anyone. As this choice was absent on the first-round survey, respondents may have felt compelled to write names down, while on the second-round survey they were given an option to have an out-degree of zero. The growth of the provider network in contrast to the other networks is impressive in spite of this potential shortcoming in the data collection.

9. In order to examine the overlap between the five networks, Jaccard coefficients were calculated. The Jaccard coefficient is the proportion of ties that are common to any two networks as compared with the total number of ties that occurred in either network.

10. In an attempt to link communication to attitude change, individual attitude change was regressed on individual density changes in the provider network using a multilevel model. Only 12.3% of the variance in attitude scores was due to between-school differences, while 87.7% was due to within-school differences among teachers. A positive and statistically significant estimate was noted

for the change in individually reported out-degree in the provider network as related to attitude change. This result implies that increased levels of ego-network size (the number of individuals with whom a teacher converses) in the provider network were associated with an individual's improved attitude toward the reform. However, in aggregating all of the school data into one single model, the results for each school are obscured, thereby meriting further investigation.

11. The directionality of the analysis also may be an issue here. Improved attitudes about the provider may encourage individuals to communicate about the program.

12. Implementation analyses were not possible for FTF1, for which we have two rounds of survey data, because the survey items regarding classroom behavior were altered from the first data collection point to the second.

REFERENCES

Agapitova, N. (2003, June). *The impact of social networks on innovation and industrial development: Social dimensions of industrial dynamics in Russia.* Paper presented at DRUID Summer Conference, Copenhagen, Denmark.

Brass, D. J. (1985). Men's and women's networks: A study of interaction patterns and influence in an organization. *Academy of Management Journal, 28*(2), 327–343.

Brown, J. S., & Duguid, P. (1991). Organizational learning and communities-of-practice: Toward a unified view of working, learning, and innovation. *Organization Science, 2*(1), 40–57.

Castells, M. (1996). *The information age: Economy, society, and culture: Vol. 1. The rise of the network society.* Oxford: Blackwell.

Coburn, C. E. (2003). Rethinking scale: Moving beyond numbers to deep and lasting change. *Educational Researcher, 32*(6), 3–12.

Coleman, J. S. (1986). Social theory, social research and theory of action. *American Journal of Sociology, 91*(6), 1309–1335.

Darling-Hammond, L., & McLaughlin, M. W. (1995). Policies that support professional development in an era of reform. *Phi Delta Kappan, 76*(8), 597–604.

Degenne, A., & Forse, M. (1999). *Introducing social networks.* London: Sage.

DuFour, R. (1999). Taking on loneliness. *Journal of Staff Development, 20*(1), 61–62.

Erickson, B. H. (1988). The relational basis of attitudes. In B. Wellman & S. D. Berkowitz (Eds.), *Social structures: A network approach* (pp. 99–121). Cambridge, England: Cambridge University Press.

Frank, K. A., & Fahrbach, K. (1999). Organizational culture as a complex system: Balance and information in models of influence and selection. *Organization Science on Chaos and Complexity, 10*(3), 253–277.

Frank, K. A., Zhao, Y., & Borman, K. (2004). Social capital and the diffusion of innovations within organizations: The case of computer technology in schools. *Sociology of Education, 77*(2), 148–171.

Homans, G. (1950). *The human group*. New York: Harcourt Brace.

Lortie, D. C. (2002). *Schoolteacher: A sociological study*. Chicago: University of Chicago Press.

Louis, K. S., Marks, H. M., & Kruse, S. (1996). Teachers' professional community in restructuring schools. *American Educational Research Journal, 33*(4), 757–798.

McLaughlin, M. W., & Talbert, J. E. (2001). *Professional communities and the work of high school teaching*. Chicago: University of Chicago Press.

Organisation for Economic Cooperation and Development. (2003). *Networks of innovation: Towards new models for managing schools and systems*. Paris: OECD Publications Service.

Siskin, L. (1994). *Realms of knowledge: Academic departments in secondary schools*. London: Falmer.

Stodolsky, S. S., & Grossman, P. L. (1995). The impact of subject matter on curricular activity: An analysis of five academic subjects. *American Educational Research Journal, 32*(2), 227–249.

Supovitz, J. A. (2002). Developing communities of practice. *Teachers College Record, 104*(8), 1591–1626.

Turner, J. (1988). *A theory of social interaction*. Stanford: University of Stanford Press.

van Duijn, M. A. J., Snijders, T. A. B., & Zijlstra, B. J. (2004). P2: Random effects model with covariates for directed graphs. *Statistica Neerlandica, 58*(2), 234–254.

Warren, L. L., & Muth, K. D. (1995). The impact of common planning time on middle grades students and teachers. *Research in Middle Level Education Quarterly, 18*(3), 41–58.

Weinbaum, E. H., Supovitz, J. A., Gross, B., Cole, R. P., Weiss, M. J., & Ricalde, B. (2006, April). *Going with the flow: Communication and reform in high schools*. Paper presented at the annual meeting of the American Educational Research Association, San Francisco.

Zeichner, K., & Gore, S. (1989). *Teacher socialization* (Working Paper). East Lansing: Michigan State University, National Center for Research on Teacher Learning.

CHAPTER 5

Interpreting, Supporting, and Resisting Change: The Geography of Leadership in Reform Settings

Matthew Riggan and Jonathan A. Supovitz

DRAWING ON extensive interview and survey data, this chapter explores the role of leadership in the enactment of the five external school reforms in the 15 high schools in this study. Building on a distributed leadership perspective, we argue that three types of leaders influence the implementation of reforms. *Traditional-formal leaders* (administrative leadership positions present within and familiar to most schools) integrate reforms into the wider agenda for the school and create pressure or incentives for teachers to adopt reform practices. *Provider-formal leaders* (leadership positions created by the reforms themselves) disseminate information about the reform, provide follow-up technical assistance and support for reform components, and facilitate communication among teachers, administrators, and in some cases provider staff. *Informal leaders* (individuals who hold no formal position but are identified as influential by their colleagues) are central in determining whether reforms gain traction within schools. Our findings suggest that

- Leadership in the enactment of external reforms is *distributed*: It is a form of activity that is carried out by multiple actors within the school, including teachers, principals, and others.
- Distributed leadership is best understood as an *organizational condition* of schools rather than a process to be undertaken by school

> leaders. Interventions focused on introducing new processes may overlook, or even undermine, existing leadership practices or configurations.

The connection between leadership and school effectiveness, although indirect, is well-established in the research literature (Hallinger & Heck, 1998; Leithwood, 2005). Traditionally, studies of educational leadership have limited their focus almost exclusively to the work of principals (Southworth, 2002). More recently, research has suggested that rather than being the sole province of school administrators, leadership is actually a distributed practice. The work of schools is accomplished through the efforts of multiple individuals, each of whom enacts a leadership role based on tasks that need to be accomplished (Spillane, Halverson, & Diamond, 2004). Gronn (2002) refers to such leadership as "concertive action"—influence is strengthened and consolidated through collaboration among multiple "leaders." Recent research suggests that distributed leadership is critical to the success of school reform efforts. Reviewing the role of leadership in the implementation of 10 comprehensive school reforms, Murphy and Datnow (2004) asserted that structures that moved "beyond positional conceptions of leadership" were central to the successful implementation of reforms, and argued for a view of leadership situated in activity rather than organizational position.

The emergence of distributed leadership theory is an important and useful development, but like most breakthroughs it presents us with new puzzles even as it helps to solve older ones. One dilemma is that while it is useful and appropriate to consider how leadership frequently is enacted through activity rather than organizational position, this does not change the fact that the context in which such activity is carried out—the geography of leadership—is shaped by formal arrangements. The formal organization of leadership influences (and is influenced by) this activity. A second problem is that distributed leadership theory is not easily "translated" into practice. Like so many professional learning community initiatives, interventions designed around the theory of distributed leadership run the risk of replacing powerful, organic leadership processes and arrangements with artificial, bureaucratic contrivances (Hargreaves & Fink, 2006).

In this chapter we both build upon and depart from distributed leadership theories. Like most distributed leadership approaches, this chapter explores how the work of leadership involves multiple actors within schools and is generally activity-based. The activity considered in our analysis is the set of tasks and interactions associated with the implementation of external school reforms. Unlike most distributed leadership analyses, however, we focus on how formal leadership arrangements influence (and are influenced by) the context in which leadership is distributed. We argue that the continuum that runs between formal and informal leadership powerfully influences the ways in which distributed leadership is enacted.

The next three sections explore the different types of leadership described above: traditional-formal, provider-formal, and informal. Using interview and survey data, we detail the role of each type in furthering (and sometimes undermining) the work of reform. A fourth section explores the interaction of these different types of leadership, while our conclusion focuses on the implications of our findings for distributed leadership theory and leadership practice.

TRADITIONAL-FORMAL LEADERSHIP

Traditional-formal leaders are defined as those in administrative positions within schools, such as principals and assistant principals. In a handful of cases, this category included administrators who were employed as district staff but were based in the schools.

This group of leaders exerted a profound influence over the process of implementing the external school improvement programs. They did so in two ways. First, they established the agenda for reform, sometimes altering the reforms in the process. Second, they created pressure or incentive to adopt the changes required by the reform. In cases where traditional-formal leaders did *not* engage in either of these activities, reform implementation was almost always superficial or limited to a small group of teachers.

Before we discuss the particular ways in which traditional-formal leaders influenced reform enactment, it is important to note that the five reforms included in this study assumed or required different behaviors and responsibilities from traditional-formal leaders, especially school administrators. The reforms also varied in the degree to which they sought to directly influence the practice of these individuals through professional development, technical assistance, or other supports.[1] While noting that such variation exists, we focus on cross-cutting behaviors that appeared to influence the enactment process.

Establishing the Agenda for Reform

Traditional-formal leaders were instrumental in determining the degree to which reforms were viewed as a high priority in their schools. This had implications for both the spread of reform and the degree to which teachers saw it as affecting them. In cases where leaders did not make the reform a high priority, there was less sense among teachers that adopting reform practices was required. For example, at RU2 and HSTW2, principals clearly communicated that reform enactment was a schoolwide priority. "What we've done is tried to unify everything . . . High Schools That Work is kind of the centerpiece, but the small learning communities, the professional learning communities, all just fit in so well," said one HSTW2 administrator. Similarly, one RU2 administrator said:

> I do believe in [Ramp-Up]. I want everybody to be able to speak the same language. So if you interview my PE teacher, he ought to be able to have an idea—that's all I'm asking for is an idea of what Ramp-Up is about. Try to improve reading.

By contrast, some administrators admitted playing a very small role in implementing the reform. They did not indicate any opposition to it, nor did they take an active stand in promoting its adoption by teachers. For example, at PLN1 and SN3, principals suggested that they played a small or no role in reform implementation, knew little about the reform, and left the decision about whether to participate up to individual teachers. Teachers suggested that principals' priorities greatly influenced their commitment to implementing the reform. At RU3, for example, the administration reportedly proposed eliminating the 90-minute block schedule, a structural staple of the reform. Teachers interpreted this as a signal that the administration was not fully committed to the reform, and suggested that other initiatives closely tied to funding opportunities had become more important to the administration than RU.

In defining the reform agenda for their schools, traditional-formal leaders sometimes altered the reforms. This appeared to happen in both intended and unintended ways. In some instances, leaders consciously chose to modify or selectively implement reform components or practices. We found evidence of such modifications in four of eight schools for which leadership tasks were defined.[2] During the planning year at FTF1, for example, the principal made significant changes to both the academic and advisory components of the reform. First, the roll-out of the reform was modified in accordance with the principal's priorities. Specifically, the instructional components of the reform were not considered as high a priority as the organizational ones, because in the early stages of adoption the principal was concerned primarily with school climate. As one FTF1 administrator noted of FTF's curricular support, "I'm not sure that's where we need the help. . . . It's the organization piece." Second, the curriculum for the family advocacy system (FTF's advisory component) was judged not to be well-matched to students' needs and was rewritten. In the process, this component was transformed from a program intended to build relationships to one geared toward college readiness. The FTF1 principal explained the rationale underlying this change:

> The family advocacy piece is very difficult. . . . Family advocacy activities . . . they're not particularly appropriate to our population. . . . So we discovered pretty early on that this just was not going to make it, so we spent a lot of time developing our own stuff. . . . You can only do so much "getting to know you" activities.

Leaders also unintentionally altered the makeup of the reforms by not recognizing the reforms' implications for their own practice. While we found several cases in which the behavior of traditional-formal leaders was *consistent* with the demands or assumptions of the reforms, we also discovered that leaders seldom *changed* their behavior in response to the reforms. For example, reforms that called for instructional engagement from principals were altered when principals failed to assume such a role. Despite the fact that the reforms required some measure of instructional leadership, administrators at PLN1, PLN2, HSTW3, and SN3 all described a hands-off approach to instruction, deferring to teachers, department chairs, or district staff on instructional decisions. In all but one of these schools, teachers suggested that the reform was not a high priority in their school.

Similarly, reforms that required leaders to be collaborative and share decision making changed significantly when administrators proved unwilling or unable to do so. Traditional-formal leaders with a more directive style did not become more collaborative through implementation, nor did those who were collaborative become more directive in accordance with reform expectations. At HSTW1, for example, few teachers felt that they had real influence on decisions made by the administration, despite the reform's expectation that teachers be heavily involved in planning and decision making. One HSTW1 teacher noted:

> I think in most situations, you know, the people at the top like to believe it's driven by their population. It's driven by their teachers . . . but I don't think so. I think it's still a top-down design for the most part, it starts at the top and then you try to get your faculty involved. . . . We do have a committee through High Schools That Works that I'm on . . . but the administration is still going to bend it and mold it to what kind of fits their needs.

While acknowledging the need to engage teachers and eventually win their support, administrators suggested that in some cases it was necessary to push beyond teachers' comfort levels in order to bring about change. An HSTW1 administrator commented:

> You'll hear probably some comments that we're dictating some things. Well, we've said, we're moving ahead. . . . And sometimes we work together, but sometimes we have to be the ones that still keep the kids in mind if you don't see that vision. And some of them still don't see that vision. But we just keep moving ahead and trying to make them see that.

In sum, by prioritizing or downplaying reform, selectively adopting or modifying reform components, and reshaping the reforms to be consistent with their own practice, traditional-formal leaders "translated" the strategies for change prescribed by the reform into a local agenda for the school. It was this local adaptation, rather than the reform as designed by its creators, that most often was implemented at the school level.

Creating Pressure or Incentive to Change

Traditional-formal leaders created pressure or incentive for teachers to adopt reform practices in a variety of ways. The most direct of these was a "my way or the highway" approach where the faculty was issued an ultimatum: Go along with reform or find another school. This message was sent explicitly in three schools. In a fourth, administrators went out of their way to note that their job was not "to make teachers happy" but rather to support students. A teacher at HSTW2 described how this message was conveyed:

> The teachers . . . are looked on by our administration as the enemy. In fact, we are told that if we can't get on the bus, then we need to get off. . . . If we go in to him [the principal] and talk to him and try to sit down and reason together, that's where the nonlistening comes. If you don't like to do it this way, get off the bus.

A second strategy used to create pressure was to emphasize the need for the school to comply with district or state policy. Traditional-formal leaders who adopted this approach could justify being assertive in mandating teacher compliance while maintaining a degree of solidarity with the teachers, as both were, in essence, being told what to do by the district or state.

A third approach was to emphasize the problems and needs of the school, and to present the reform as an appropriate and useful response. Central to this strategy was the process of building consensus around the need for teachers to change what they did in the classroom. One SN1 administrator observed:

> Our math scores in 11th grade are 4% proficient for Caucasian kids, and 8% proficient for African-American kids. . . . So they've been in school since kindergarten, and they're not learning math skills? . . . If teachers were teaching differently—I think what they do is reteach the same thing, the same way, harder maybe . . . I just don't think teachers know what exactly to do.

A fourth strategy for creating incentive to change was to confer greater autonomy, decision-making authority, or status on those teachers who were most active in the reform. At RU2, school and district leaders worked to create a "buzz" around RU, even using the reform as a tool to recruit new teachers. Successes of RU teachers were highlighted, heightening their visibility within the school and broadening teacher interest in the reform. Together, these efforts served to increase teacher engagement in RU while building trust and confidence in leadership. One RU2 teacher commented, "I don't think there's a teacher in the school that doesn't know [RU's] success. I mean—we have even had discussions online: How can we apply this to different areas academically?" Another RU2 teacher said:

> The climate here has changed so much that we believe what the administration was telling us. And it was [the principal] and the way he set up—it wasn't just one person or the district telling us we're going to do this.

At HSTW2, the principal convened a small group of teachers who supported the reform, and frequently consulted with them before making decisions. In doing so, he attempted to confer authority upon those in the school who shared his view of reform, in essence spreading his influence.

Where traditional-formal leaders did *not* create pressure or incentive to change, in most cases implementation was superficial or limited to a small group of teachers. At SN2 and SN3, for example, low levels of use of SN applications appeared to be directly related to the principals' reluctance to emphasize the importance of the reform. At two of the three PLN schools, implementation was limited to a small number of teachers who volunteered to participate. While this is in accordance with the reform's traditional design (as discussed in Chapter 3), it is worth noting that at PLN3, where PLN was implemented as a whole-school reform, the traditional-formal leaders played an active role in facilitating teacher engagement.

PROVIDER-FORMAL LEADERSHIP

Provider-formal leaders[3] filled positions called for by the reforms for the express purpose of facilitating some aspect of implementation. These leaders functioned as the link between the reforms and classrooms. In some instances this link was somewhat weak; leaders simply relayed information from the district or provider to a group of teachers. In other cases the link was much stronger, with provider-formal leaders working to champion reform ideas, build the capacity of teachers to adopt reform practices, address concerns or grievances, and advocate for teachers as they worked to integrate reforms in their classrooms.

As with traditional-formal leaders, the role of provider-formal leaders varied considerably across the five reforms. Three of the reforms (FTF, HSTW, and RU) called for the creation of strategically important provider-formal roles.[4] In the other two reforms (PLN and SN), provider-formal positions were not clearly defined and were less central to implementation. Across all reforms, however, provider-formal leadership mattered. At the most basic level, provider-formal leaders disseminated reform information to teachers, usually through meetings, professional development, or distribution of materials. At all three SN schools, for example, department chairs or technology coordinators participated in SN professional development at the district level, and then led SN trainings for teachers in their schools. At PLN1 and PLN2, district staff or department chairs served as "point persons" for the reform; their primary role was coordinating logistics for PLN courses.

In schools implementing FTF, HSTW, and RU, provider-formal leaders' roles were considerably more expansive. In addition to technical or operational responsibilities, these leaders often served as champions for the reform and advocates for the teachers adopting it.

At an operational level, implementation of FTF, HSTW, and RU relied on a multilevel professional development model that included both off-site and school-based training and support. In FTF, this was reflected in a combination of direct and turnkey training, while HSTW and RU combined direct professional development with school-level follow-up. Regardless of the professional development model, provider-formal leaders were instrumental in delivering school-based supports. Thus, they were chiefly responsible for supporting the adoption of reform practices at the classroom level. Provider-formal leaders sought to address this critical need in three ways. First, they led school-based professional development around the reforms. In FTF, for example, this occurred at two levels. School improvement facilitators (SIFs) participated in off-site professional development from the provider and then delivered training to small learning community (SLC) coordinators. Second, some provider-formal leaders offered instructional coaching for teachers adopting reform practices. In some RU schools, literacy coaches conducted regular observations of RU teachers, modeled the reform's instructional practices, and facilitated meetings with teachers to discuss their challenges and successes with the RU curriculum. Third, provider-formal leaders facilitated teacher conversations about themes and topics related to reform implementation. In HSTW schools, focus team leaders were responsible not only for sharing information about the reform but for organizing teacher meetings to discuss reform components. The focus team leaders set goals and expectations for group meetings, defined roles to be played by the participants, and worked to invite all teachers into the conversation, increasing engagement and participation.

Beyond these operational tasks, there appeared to be a more affective dimension to provider-formal leaders' work. On the one hand, they were frequently champions for the reform at the school level. For example, teachers at FTF2 described the SIF as the catalyst for change in the school. One teacher commented, "If she leaves, I have not a clue. She has been at the forefront . . . for making sure that everything is done. She's the lone star." For her part, the SIF described her role as pushing teachers to improve their instruction, citing accountability pressures.

> What is my strategy? I don't have a major strategy other than my encouraging speech, which turns into, "Okay, fine. When they take over the school, you're going to be looking for a job." . . . You get paid every two weeks, I need you to do the job. . . . We got to help those kids pass. We've got to do this. . . . We need to do something. We need to shake something up.

On the other hand, provider-formal leaders also played an important part in advocating on behalf of teachers to school administrators or provider staff. In most FTF and HSTW schools, teachers and administrators alike noted that the most effective provider-formal leaders (SIFs, SLC coordinators, and focus team leaders) were good listeners, responded quickly to teacher needs or requests, and served as the teachers' voices with the administration or provider. An SLC coordinator at FTF1 noted:

> Just being someone that people can trust, I think that's a big deal that they know, yes—It's kind of like I'm in between. Yes, I'm with the administrators, you know in a certain way, but then I'm also one of them. I'm a teacher just like they are so they know they can come to me with their concerns and I'll bring their concerns. So they trust me enough to bring their concerns to the administration.

In sum, provider-formal leaders supported reform implementation on multiple levels. While their operational responsibilities, such as relaying information and supporting teacher adoption of reform practices, were critical, their effectiveness frequently depended on their capacity to maintain good relationships with both teachers and administrators, and to serve as an advocate for each with the other.

INFORMAL LEADERSHIP

> I think we all have leadership times and capabilities. When I need to provide services I would say yes [I am a leader], but I don't spend my day trying to organize as a leader. (Teacher, FTF1)

The statement above encapsulates a dimension of organizational leadership that often goes unnoticed, yet is central to a robust picture of the full range of leadership activity in schools. This requires investigation beyond the efforts of those who hold formal leadership roles into the leadership acts of those who do not hold formal leadership positions. The extent of leadership activity by teachers and other school actors is an important contributing factor in why some reforms gain traction while other efforts never take root. Informal leaders play important and distinctive roles in determining the extent to which reforms reach deeply into schools and influence instructional practice. Their efforts provide a different type of support for reforms than that provided by either traditional-formal or provider-formal leaders. They may either complement or weaken the hold of a reform in a school. Informal leaders can act as glue in bonding a reform to an environment or they can act as a solvent, weakening the hold of a reform.

Instructional leadership consists of a range of activities that support teachers' efforts to engage students with subject-matter content and measurably improve their learning. Researchers typically view instructional leadership as the activities and efforts of formal school leaders. For example, Gordon (1997) described the prevailing conception of instructional leadership as one of inspection, oversight, and judgment of classroom instruction. Others define instructional leadership as the action of assisting teachers to improve their instruction, such as direct assistance to teachers through group development, staff development, curriculum development, or action research (Glickman, 1985). Pajak (1989) viewed it as planning, organizing and facilitating change, and motivating staff. Schön (1988) conceptualized instructional leadership as the support, guidance, and encouragement of reflective teaching.

While many of these perspectives on the actions of instructional leaders characterize what formal leaders do, they just as easily could describe the actions of instructional supporters, regardless of position. In fact, analyses of the survey data from this study indicate that instructional support and influence are more likely to come from teachers than from formal leaders (Riggan & Supovitz, 2006; Supovitz, 2008). In our survey, teachers were asked whom they sought assistance from in three areas of professional concern (course content and planning, classroom management, and assisting low-performing students) as well as about the provider. Responses were analyzed to identify those individuals who were significantly more likely to be recipients of requests for assistance than would occur by chance.[5] For issues of course content and planning, two thirds of the individuals who were identified as influential were teachers who held no formal leadership position. For questions about classroom management issues, 56% of those who were significantly influential were teachers, while 15% were department chairs, and 18% were school administrators. For information about assisting low-performing students, 64% of those who were recipients of requests for assistance were teachers, not formal school leaders.[6] These data indicate that a subset of teachers clearly were playing influential roles with their peers in terms of providing assistance around issues of instructional improvement.

Based on these findings, we sought to understand the ways in which informal leaders viewed themselves within the context of their schools and how they influenced reform efforts. (See the appendix in this chapter for a description of the methods used to identify and sample leaders for this study.) Relevant to these questions, we asked these individuals how they saw their role in the school and whether they considered themselves to be leaders in the school for either instruction or for deepening the school's reform efforts. We also asked them whether their school had informal leaders—which we defined as those who provided support and were influential while not holding formal leadership positions—and what they thought were the qualities of those informal leaders.

Through our analyses, several themes emerged that distinguish both the role and influence of informal leadership in schools in contrast to that of traditional- and provider-formal leaders:

1. Informal leaders think of themselves as problem solvers whose efforts arise out of tasks that need to be addressed.
2. Informal leaders deepen reforms because they have "in the trenches" experience with the reform that is distinctive from the training expertise that provider-formal leaders have.

3. Informal leaders have a currency with some of their peers precisely because they do not hold formal positions in the organization; their "outsider" status gives them legitimacy.
4. Informal leaders sometimes can provide resources more efficiently than can be received through formal requests.
5. Informal leadership can arise out of dysfunction in formal organizational leadership.
6. In some circumstances, informal leaders can act in opposition to reform, weakening reform introduction into schools.

We discuss these findings in greater detail in the following sections.

Solving Problems

First, and surprisingly, few of the informal leaders that we interviewed thought of themselves as leaders. Rather, they described their leadership activities as arising out of what they saw as an urgent need to solve difficult problems that they and their colleagues faced. "We have so many issues that there's no time to be a leader. There's only time to solve the problems that pop up," said a teacher at FTF1. "I mean, leaders don't do anything if they don't solve problems."

This dynamic was illustrated clearly in the case of one informal leader at HSTW2. While she specifically explained that she did not see herself as a leader because she held no administrative title, she detailed a scenario in which her connection to a special needs program thrust her into something of a leadership role.

> The beginning of this school year, the first nine weeks, we had 187 failures [students who failed a class]. . . . That's a lot of failures. . . . So, I met with the principal and I said, "Okay, look, what do we need to do about this?" . . . And I don't really have anyone saying, "Okay, this is what you need to do." I have to devise the way to. . . . In the plan, I had to come up with how our school was restructuring our [student support] teams, and restructuring how we were going to do [student support] in our school. So, I was pretty much having to take the initiative to do that and get it organized, to get it moving along. So, I would say in that aspect, yes, that would be more of a leadership role.

Several teachers acknowledged the extra commitment that was necessary in taking on informal leadership tasks. "So you see these leaders arise not because they have the title, but because they're willing to do it and they want to put more time in," said a teacher at FTF1. Informal leaders "gain that status based upon the way they are presented problems and come up with solutions."

Deepening Reforms

Second, findings from our data indicated that informal leaders deepen reforms because they have experience with the reform that is distinctive from the training expertise that provider-formal leaders have. The influence of informal leaders arose from their credibility as effective teachers in their schools. Both teachers and informal leaders alike described instructional expertise as a central reason for the authority of informal leaders. Asked why a particular informal leader might be influential, one HSTW2 teacher cited that person's recognized expertise in assessment strategies.

> I'll give her the scenario, [and] she'll do research on that kind of assessment to see who else had success or failure with it, and she'll bring back some proof, so to speak. Or she will think, and think, and think, and then come back with an alternative. . . . We rely on her for all research, analysis, interpretation of numbers. We all offer our opinion, but she's the one that really studies it.

Asked a general question about how two specific teachers seemed to earn the respect of their colleagues, one HSTW2 teacher cited instructional expertise and rapport with students as key ingredients.

> She is just so professional and takes her job so seriously. . . . [It] is all about the betterment of the kids. And they've been here . . . a while and they're very much respected. . . . I think a lot of it has to do with their rapport with the students. Again, kids know if you care about them. They know if you care about their personal issues as well as their academic issues. And I feel like these two teachers do. And, you know, word gets around.

In our interviews, the informal leaders gave several examples of how they took initiative to work with colleagues to deepen, and in some cases modify, different components of the reform that was being implemented in their school. For example, a teacher at FTF1 described how he was working with other teachers to develop cross-disciplinary projects. His description indicated that he was not just coordinating his project but involving himself in (and loosely directing) those of others in the SLC. In another example, an informal leader at FTF1 was taking ownership of the family advocacy system by coordinating all members of the SLC, in addition to students' assigned family advocates, to meet together with the parents of students regarding discipline and/or academic issues. By doing this, the teacher was adapting the reform even as she acted to deepen it in the school.

Legitimacy as "Outsiders"

A third point that arose from our analyses suggested that informal leaders have legitimacy with some of their peers precisely because they do not hold formal positions in the organization. Several informal leaders felt that their influence was at least in part due to the comfort level associated with their lack of advisory or evaluative capacity. A teacher at HSTW1 who was identified by our survey as an informal leader said:

> I get a lot of newer teachers that will come to me and ask for just general information. . . . I think that is a situation where you're new in the building, you don't want to go talk to somebody who's in a higher up position, so it's easier to go to somebody who's just been here a while.

Others associated accessibility with seeking assistance from informal leaders. When asked why she preferred to ask peers to answer her questions, one teacher at FTF1 explained, "They're more familiar, it's easier to go to that person because you see that person every day and know them." She explained how questions for the reading specialist required meetings, "whereas if I'm asking the people that I'm thinking about, these things, I'm going to walk a couple of doors down and they are right there, and it's going to be real comfortable."

Providing Resources Efficiently

Fourth, our interviews with informal leaders suggested that informal leaders sometimes can provide resources more efficiently than more formal systems. School systems, like many large organizations, often become bureaucratic in the way they distribute resources. Informal leaders sometimes arose due to their ability to provide alternative means for teachers to gain access to the materials they needed. For instance, a teacher at FTF1 who was cited persistently by his peers as an informal leader in the school explained how problems sometimes were addressed more efficiently by avoiding the formal system: "There are channels and there are channels.

And when a person needs to get something done, you do what you need to do. There's all different ways that one employs in order to try to solve problems." He then gave an example of how a new teacher in his building wanted to do a project and needed to get supplies.

> They could have gone to the administration and put in a requisition and perhaps they may get or may not get what they needed. Or they could use other ways to get what they need through their colleagues. . . . If [they] get the job done and get on with the other problems of running [their] day, that would be the most logical way for [them] to approach the problem.

Filling a Leadership Vacuum

Fifth, there were situations in which informal leadership arose out of dysfunction in formal organizational leadership. There were several instances in our data in which informal leaders, recognizing a vacuum in formal school leadership, stepped in to take charge of needed tasks. One HSTW2 teacher explained how rapid leadership turnover resulted in something of a vacuum that ultimately was filled by informal leaders.

> And having so many changes and having different principals . . . I think a lot of things have got, just kind of gotten lost. There's not a lot of continuity as far as consistency . . . the administrators are just trying to keep up. . . . I know there's a few key people that are not in leadership roles, I think, that give information or try to show a leadership role, or I'm not even real sure how to explain it. . . . I just think that they voice their opinions and their views. And then when the administrators, they accept their views and their, I guess, professional judgment or whatever you want to call it, and decisions are made that affect the whole school.

Weakening Reform

Finally, examples from our data indicated that, in some circumstances, informal leaders acted in opposition to reform, weakening reform implementation in schools. For example, one teacher in an HSTW school who was nominated as influential by peers in multiple areas talked about his opposition to the reform, suggesting that "80% of the faculty" were against it. His criticism of a specific reform component illustrated how he was in a position to undermine reform implementation.

> Well, the big goal [of the component] is to make the students feel as if someone's there that they can come and talk to, and so on and so forth. Well, if the teachers don't want it, what makes you think that they're going to want to work with these kids? The students don't want it. . . . I think [it's] a waste of time . . . I mean, the kids in my . . . group, they keep on asking, "What is the point of this?" And I hate to say it but people are going out the door and I'm saying, "I really don't know myself."

In sum, informal leadership arose both from individual motivation and organizational circumstance. Those who enacted informal leadership did so because they saw themselves as being in a position to help solve problems for students, colleagues, and/or the school (although for some informal leaders, as noted before, the reform itself might be the problem). In so doing, they took on extra tasks and additional responsibilities that embodied informal leadership, regardless of any recognition they may have received. While informal leadership undoubtedly was individually motivated, it also arose from organizational situations. Opportunities for informal leadership expanded when formal leaders were either deficient in their responsibilities, unresponsive to the requests of faculty members, or in some cases deliberately hands-off in their approach. Insofar as they emerged both in support of and in opposition to traditional-formal leadership, informal leaders were both constructive and destructive to reform efforts.

INTERACTION AMONG LEADERSHIP TYPES

The three types of leadership described in this chapter interacted in several ways. First, there were numerous cases in which informal leaders assumed provider-formal positions as reforms were adopted. At PLN3, for example, the initial introduction of PLN was facilitated by two teachers who were enthusiastic supporters of the reform. In response to a state policy requiring the adoption of a whole-school reform, these individuals, working with school and district administrators and their peers, successfully advocated for the reform to be modified (in partnership with the provider) to meet state-mandated, whole-school reform requirements. These two teachers and informal leaders naturally assumed provider-formal leadership roles as point people for PLN, coordinating communication and logistics in the implementation process.

Second, traditional-formal leaders often recruited informal leaders to fill provider-formal positions. For example, one teacher at FTF1 noted:

> I think a lot of those informal leaders were put into formal leadership positions. They became the SLC chairs, the SLC coordinators. . . . So I think part of the implementation was to recognize who those people were and take advantage of their willingness or the fact they'd already had some leadership credibility.

Not surprisingly, this relationship allowed traditional-formal leaders to profoundly influence the work of provider-formal leaders. Across schools and reforms, provider-formal leaders cited their relationship with school administrators as a critical factor supporting or undermining their work.

Third, in some schools, administrators assimilated provider-formal roles into their own, or sought to modify those roles in accordance with their own agenda. At FTF3, for example, the principal assumed the SIF role, while at HSTW1 and HSTW2, principals also served as site coordinators. In other cases, administrators defined provider-formal roles in ways that served their own ends. During the planning year at FTF1, the principal and SIF struggled to work together, in part because the lines of authority between them were seen as unclear. The SIF ultimately moved to another school and was replaced by someone who reported directly to the principal.

Finally, in a handful of cases, traditional-formal leaders appeared to inadvertently facilitate the emergence of informal leadership in the form of resistance. This was evident in at least three schools, where resistance to reform emerged primarily from resentment of formal leaders themselves. This resistance produced specific constituencies that in turn gave rise to informal leaders.

CONCLUSION

The work of implementing reforms was spread across three types of leadership, each of which played a vital role in the process. In most cases, schools that made significant progress on implementation received meaningful contributions from leaders of all types.

In some respects, our findings paralleled existing research on leadership. The role of traditional-formal leaders, for example, was consistent with much of the literature on leading organizational change. Setting the agenda for change closely parallels calls for leaders to craft and communicate a vision for the organization. Similarly, creating pressure or incentives to change echoes recommendations to mobilize staff commitment, establish a sense of urgency, or regulate the level of comfort or discomfort in order to push the need for change (Beer, Eisenstat, & Spector, 1990; Heifetz & Laurie, 1997; Kotter, 1995).

In our analysis, we also found consistencies with some of the existing literature on distributed leadership. Specifically, we found that the work of enacting reform consisted of a series of tasks, that leadership around these tasks was "stretched" across multiple actors, and that leadership was enacted collaboratively (Gronn, 2002; Spillane et al., 2004).

At the same time, our analysis suggests that while leadership may be distributed around specific tasks or activities, the manner in which those tasks are framed, understood, and carried out is profoundly influenced by organizational position. As such, position and activity are intertwined. Different types of leaders serve different functions, which shape their engagement in various reform tasks. Informal leaders play an especially important, and often overlooked, role in legitimizing reforms and supporting changes in classroom practice. This role is not merely task-driven; the type of support provided by informal leaders is a function of their position within the formal organization. In sum, the organization of leadership in schools directly shapes the work of reform and is thus a central component in understanding how leadership is distributed in reform settings.

Our findings also underscore Hargreaves and Fink's (2006) admonition that "no one needs to distribute leadership; it's already distributed" (p. 136). Our findings suggest that distributed leadership is best thought of as an *organizational condition* of schools, rather than an intervention to be imposed upon them. Given the importance of distributed leadership to reform success, we understand the interest among reformers and policymakers in developing strategies for cultivating distributed leadership structures and practices in schools. We suggest, however, that any such intervention must begin with an exploration of how leadership is distributed organically (i.e., pre-intervention) and build from there. Our research suggests that reforms that start from the assumption that distributed leadership is merely an act of unilateral delegation, or can be facilitated simply by creating new decision-making structures, are likely to overlook, or even disempower, highly influential individuals within schools and thus undermine the very distribution they aim to facilitate.

It is also important to note that while this research offers some new insights into how distributed leadership is enacted, it also has some limitations and raises some questions that are, as of yet, unanswered. First, the positional analysis presented here is incomplete. In any school, there are positions within the organizational structure that involve leadership roles or capacities. Among the schools in this study, for example, department chairs played important roles in some schools and were "glorified secretaries" (to use one chair's term) in others. The same might be said of other positions, such as deans or guidance counselors. Second, the "geography" of leadership that we posit here is likely more complex than our analysis reflects. Specifically, our research suggests that there is a powerful historical dimension to the leadership types presented in our analysis. For example, it seems entirely plausible that through successful reform implementation, provider-formal leaders might be transferred into traditional-formal roles that could outlive the reforms themselves. As noted by historians Tyack and Cuban (1997), reforms come in waves and leave a "sedimentary" layer in their wake. These layers reflect an influence on the geography of leadership in ways that transcend specific reform efforts.

Finally, while we theorize an interaction between different types of leadership, we can say little about the ways in which formal and informal leadership actually influence each other. We might hypothesize, for example, that informal leaders play an important role in legitimizing formal leaders, or in counteracting resistance to reform. Similarly, it seems likely that a complementary relationship exists between the enactment of formal and informal leadership; the role and salience of each is shaped by the other. Further developing and testing such theories is a potential focus of future research.

APPENDIX: METHODOLOGY

In this analysis, we employed a mixed-method design combining quantitative social network analysis with qualitative analysis. Social network analysis is a methodology that quantitatively describes relationships among individuals in an organization. After the initial round of data collection, transcribed interviews were analyzed in two iterations. The first iteration organized all of the data pertaining to the enactment of leadership. A review of those data yielded a second set of analytic codes related to the process and context of assistance seeking: who was sought out for assistance, why, and to what ends. The data were then recoded using this revised set of categories.

Concurrently, the social network survey data were analyzed to identify influential individuals within each of the professional networks (course content and planning, classroom management, and strategies for assisting low-performing students, see Chapter 4) and the provider network in each school. Network survey data from each school were analyzed to identify those individuals who received high numbers of requests to provide information and assistance in each network, and to ascertain the relative influence of these contacts. This resulted in the tabulation of a "frequency-influence" score for each person. A series of statistical tests were applied to these scores to identify "significantly influential individuals" in each of the four networks. The result was a "map" of influence in each school that was derived entirely from the perspective of those seeking assistance.

These maps were used to develop a two-tiered sample for additional qualitative data collection and analysis. The first tier focused on a subset of three high schools. Interviews were conducted with individuals identified as influential in one or more of the professional networks, with specific emphasis on those individuals who did not hold formal leadership positions. Interviews focused on interviewees' roles in providing assistance to their colleagues, the context in which such interactions occurred, and their interpretations of why they were sought out by their peers. A total of 16 interviews were completed. The second tier included teachers and administrators in nine early-implementing schools.[7] Interview protocols focused on general questions of leadership, influence, and authority. All interviews were subsequently transcribed and coded.

Two types of survey items focused on the frequency and influence of interpersonal communication. First, survey responses to the frequency stem, "How often have you sought guidance from this person?" were on a 4-point scale to represent an approximate number of days in a school year ("Daily or almost daily" = 150, "Once or twice a week" = 40, "Once or twice a month" = 20, "A few times a year" = 2). Second, responses to the influence stem, "How influential is the advice . . . " were also on a 4-point scale to represent the proportion of influential conversations with respect to the respondent's practice ("Highly influential" = 100%, "Influential" = 70%, "Slightly influential" = 40%, "Not influential" = 10%). Because survey respondents were able to associate a frequency and a level of influence with the request for help, strength of the relationship was built into the survey. Thus, the ties between individuals could be transformed to contain a measure of strength, and not just a binary indicator of whether or not there was communication between a pair.

To utilize all of the survey data, we combined the frequency and influence measures by multiplying the respective scores and then taking the natural log of the result (Frank, Zhao, & Borman, 2004). A constant was added to the product before the logarithm in order to produce positive results. The logarithm was performed to reduce the positive skew of the frequency-influence product. The final weighted tie-strength metric took on 16 unique values, all in the [1,5] range. Noncommunication was assigned a weight of zero.

These measures allowed us to ascertain an average value for the organizational strength of each network, as well as the individual strength or influence of each actor in the organization. Each individual in the network was associated with an "influence" score by summing the weighted in-ties to that individual. As a result, each individual's influence score for each network was a function of the responses of everyone else in the school and was thus a proxy for peer endorsement of influence.

To identify individuals whose influence was statistically significant, we compared the actual distribution of influence with the distribution that we would expect to see by chance alone. This was accomplished by randomly assigning each individual's weighted out-ties[8] to other individuals in the network. Once all of the weighted ties had been reassigned, the influence measure for each individual was recalculated for the new random data. Both influence distributions (actual and random) were sorted, and each individual's actual score in the original dataset could be compared with the influence score of the individual of the same rank in the random dataset. Ten thousand random iterations were performed, and individuals were considered "statistically significant influentials" if their influence score was higher than their random-ranked counterpart at least 99% of the time. Thus, we were able to create a sampling distribution of influence scores that would arise by random chance given the set of survey responses, and to identify those individuals whose influence was statistically significantly greater than random chance, while holding constant the number, frequency, and influence of conversations in the network.

NOTES

1. We have explored design variation in a previous paper (Riggan & Supovitz, 2006) and will consider how alignment between reform expectations and leadership practice influences implementation progress in a separate analysis.

2. Of the five reforms in this study, PLN and SN do not specify responsibilities or tasks for school leaders. The eight schools cited here are those implementing FTF, HSTW, and RU, for which leadership roles are clearly defined.

3. For the purposes of our analysis, provider-formal positions included the school improvement facilitator and small learning community coordinators in FTF, the site coordinator and focus team leaders in HSTW, and the literacy coach in RU. In the case of PLN and SN, we included individuals who served as the primary point of contact for the reform in the school as provider-formal leaders, although their role was minimal and largely unspecified by the reforms themselves.

4. It should be noted, however, that the literacy coach position was recommended but not required by RU.

5. See Cole and Weiss (2006) for an explanation of the methodology for statistically identifying influential individuals.

6. The majority (85%) of individuals in the sample were teachers, whereas only 6% were department chairs. In addition, 5% of the individuals in the sample were school administrators. Accordingly, the procedure to identify influential individuals identified disproportionately more administrators and department chairs than teachers.

7. The full complement of 10 early-implementing schools could not be used because data collection opportunities at FTF2 were curtailed due to natural disaster and the closing of the school.

8. The number of out-ties is the number of individuals that a survey respondent names as being approached for advice in a particular network. Weighted out-ties incorporate the frequency with which each person is approached, as well as the level of influence that the person reportedly has on the person completing the survey.

REFERENCES

Beer, M., Eisenstat, R. A., & Spector, B. A. (1990). Why change programs don't produce change. *Harvard Business Review, 68*(6), 158–166.

Cole, R., & Weiss, M. (2006). *Follow the leader: Identifying organizational leaders using network data*. Unpublished manuscript.

Frank, K. A., Zhao, Y., & Borman, K. (2004). Social capital and the diffusion of innovations within organizations: The case of computer technology in schools. *Sociology of Education, 77*(2), 148–171.

Glickman, C. (1985). *Supervision of instruction: A developmental approach.* Newton, MA: Allyn & Bacon.

Gordon, S. (1997). Has the field of supervision evolved to a point that it should be called something else? In J. Glanz & R. F. Neville (Eds.), *Educational supervision: Perspectives, issues, and controversies* (pp. 114–123). Norwood, MA: Christopher-Gordon.

Gronn, P. (2002). Distributed leadership. In K. Leithwood, P. Hallinger, K. Seashore-Louis, G. Furman-Brown, P. Gronn, M. Mulford, & K. Riley (Eds.), *Second international handbook of educational leadership and administration* (pp. 653–696). Dordrecht, The Netherlands: Kluwer Academic.

Hallinger, P., & Heck, R. (1998). Exploring the principal's contribution to school effectiveness: 1980–1995. *School Effectiveness and School Improvement, 9*(2), 157–191.

Hargreaves, A., & Fink, D. (2006). *Sustainable leadership.* San Francisco: Wiley.

Heifetz, R. A., & Laurie, D. L. (1997). The work of leadership. *Harvard Business Review, 75*(1), 124–134.

Kotter, J. (1995). Leading change: Why transformation efforts fail. *Harvard Business Review, 73*(2), 59–67.

Leithwood, K. (2005). *Educational leadership: A review of the research.* Philadelphia: Mid-Atlantic Regional Educational Laboratory.

Murphy, J., & Datnow, A. (2004). *Leadership lessons from comprehensive school reforms.* Thousand Oaks, CA: Corwin Press.

Pajak, E. (1989). *Identification of supervisory proficiencies project.* Alexandria, VA: Association for Supervision and Curriculum Development.

Riggan, M., & Supovitz, J. A. (2006, April). *They come in all shapes and sizes: Leaders and high school reform efforts.* Paper presented at the annual meeting of the American Educational Research Association, San Francisco.

Schön, D. (1988). Coaching reflective teaching. In P. P. Grimmett & G. F. Erickson (Eds.), *Reflection in teacher education* (pp. 19–30). New York: Teachers College Press.

Southworth, G. (2002). Instructional leadership in schools: Reflections and empirical evidence. *School Leadership & Management, 22*(1), 73–91.

Spillane, J., Halverson, R., & Diamond, J. (2004). Towards a theory of leadership practice: A distributed perspective. *Journal of Curriculum Studies, 36*(1), 3–34.

Supovitz, J. A. (2008). Instructional influence in American high schools. In M. M. Mangin & S. R. Stoelinga (Eds.), *Effective teacher leadership using research to inform and reform.* New York: Teachers College Press.

Tyack, D., & Cuban, L. (1997). *Tinkering toward utopia: A century of public school reform.* Cambridge, MA: Harvard University Press.

CHAPTER 6

Tilting the Scales: Central Office Support for External School Reforms

Elliot H. Weinbaum, Catherine Dunn Shiffman, and Margaret E. Goertz

The role of the central office[1] in supporting school improvement efforts has expanded as local, state, and national attention increasingly focuses on school performance. In many states, the central office is now required to play a role in the first round of school improvement efforts for those schools that fail to meet targets for student performance. One way in which these offices attempt to help schools meet performance goals is by brokering relationships with external school reform organizations. Previous research has analyzed the ways in which schools and central offices search for and select external school reforms (Bodilly, Keltner, Purnell, Reichardt, & Schuyler, 1998; Gross & Goertz, 2005; Hatch, 1998). While central office staff played a role in initiating each of the 15 school–provider partnerships that form the basis of this study, search and selection are not the focus of this chapter. Instead, we focus on the period following the selection of the reform to examine the ongoing implementation and support efforts of the central office. In particular, we seek to answer two related research questions:

- What role does the central office play in supporting external school reforms?
- What explains why some central offices actively support external school reform efforts while others take a much less active role?

Previous research has shown the importance of the central office role in supporting reforms (Datnow & Stringfield, 2000). Some studies even identify key district characteristics that shape how central offices support reform enactment and use in their schools (Bodilly et al., 1998; McLaughlin & Talbert, 2003; Spillane & Thompson, 1997). For the most part, these characteristics are treated as essential elements of a district's context and identity. While we recognize that characteristics previously cited in the research, such as a strong system focus, sufficient capacity, or participatory planning processes, are helpful in determining the level of central office support, we argue that substantial central office support is not dependent on district characteristics alone, but depends instead on a "match" between district characteristics and the expectations of providers.

The hypothesis that the match between contexts and expectations influences central office support is based in part on previous research on school reform, research that does not necessarily examine the central office role. For example, Yonezawa and Datnow (1999) found that the degree of "curricular fit" at the school level influenced reforms' popularity with teachers. Although this was an ongoing process of negotiation, the initial perceptions of teachers were important ones. In studies of school reform more generally, research has settled on "a widespread understanding that finding an appropriate fit between schools and designs is crucial to success" (Hatch, 2000, p. 347). Given the combination of previous findings that the central office role is critical in supporting reform and that a match or fit between schools and reforms is also essential, we hypothesized that the match between reforms and districts is no less important than the one between reforms and schools.

By examining the concept of the match between the district context and provider expectations, we are able to explain why some central offices supported a chosen reform in their high schools, while other districts with similar characteristics, but that chose a different reform, did not support the reform in the expected manner. Figure 6.1 illustrates our argument, each element of which is described in the text that follows.

DISTRICT CHARACTERISTICS

If it is true that a match between district and reform is needed for active central office support, what are the essential dimensions on which this match must be made? Based on our hypothesis that the characteristics of supportive districts were at least half of an important story, we drew from that literature. We clustered frequently cited district characteristics into three broad themes: the *coupling* between central offices and schools, the

Figure 6.1. Theory of central office support.

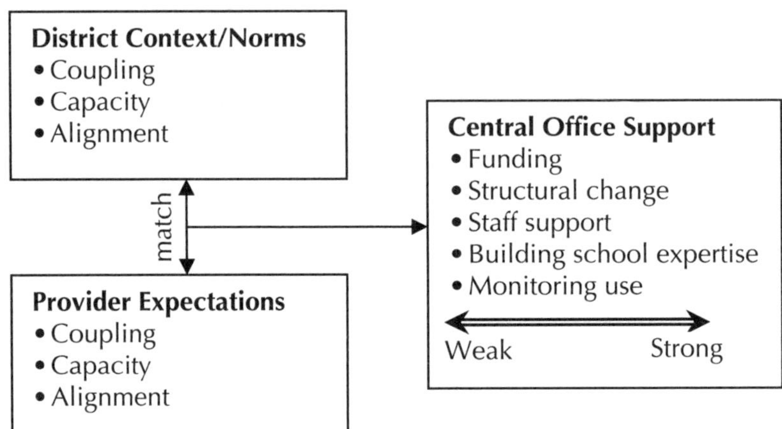

fiscal and human *capacity* of the central office, and the *alignment* of reforms and priorities within the district. These district characteristics are reviewed below.

Coupling

Research points to the central office–high school relationship and, in particular, the degree of control exercised by the central office over high school operations as an important dimension of central office support for reforms. A RAND study describes the relationship between the central office and high school in terms of the level of autonomy granted to schools over core functions, including curriculum and instruction, budget, and personnel (Bodilly et al., 1998). Kronley and Handley (2003) similarly point to the control exercised by the central office over the reform. In their research, McLaughlin and Talbert (2003) argue for a systems approach to reform and state that "reforming districts establish clear expectations for central office–school relations and *take a leadership role* in developing shared norms of reform practice across district schools" (p. 11; emphasis added). This requires what Weick (1976) called a "tightly coupled system"—one in which different levels of the system work closely together. For this reason, we discuss the central office–high school relationship in terms of its level of coupling.

Capacity

The role of local capacity in implementing reforms has long been recognized by educational researchers. Central office capacity, in particular, is considered to have three basic dimensions: financial, social capital, and human capital (Spillane & Thompson, 1997). Firestone (1989) viewed central office capacity to implement and use reforms as "the extent to which the district has the knowledge, skills, personnel, and other resources necessary to carry out decisions" (p. 157). Among these "other resources" is the degree to which human and social capital are utilized for the development of a culture of learning and trust (Bryk & Schneider, 2002) at the central office level, or what others (McLaughlin & Talbert, 2001) have called a "professional learning community." Similarly, Bodilly and colleagues (1998) point to the central office's "availability of resources for transformation" (p. 99), including costs posed by the reform, personnel, training and planning, and other materials and conferences, as important.

Alignment

Finally, the reform's relationship to district priorities and ongoing efforts influences the central office's predisposition to provide support for the reform. In this chapter, we focus on the reform's alignment with district efforts. In some cases, this means that the reform is a central feature organizing district efforts. In other cases, the reform is central only to one particular priority area or set of activities. Centrality places the reform at the core of district efforts, a placement that is not necessarily needed for reforms that target a particular area of instruction or practice, such as the two literacy reforms in this study (Penn Literacy Network and Ramp-Up). Because of these two possibilities, we choose not to use the term *centrality* in district work, as other researchers have done (Bodilly et al., 1998). Also, we do not specifically examine the significant role of leadership in aligning central office support for the reform, as discussed in other research (Bodilly et al., 1998; Corcoran & Lawrence, 2003; Kronley & Handley, 2003) and in Chapter 5 of this volume. Our focus here is on whether the reform is aligned with the district's other efforts and reform initiatives, rather than the qualities of or actions taken by individuals to facilitate or hinder this alignment process.

Where the reform is *aligned* with district priorities in such areas as curriculum and instruction, resource allocation, professional development, and assessment, we see consistency and coherence between the reform and the work of the central office (Desimone, 2002; Glennan, Bodilly,

Galegher, & Kerr, 2004; McLaughlin & Talbert, 2003). In these cases, connections between the reform and central office work are logical, frequent, and complementary. In contrast, when the reform is not aligned with district priorities in these areas, the central office must decide among competing efforts and responsibilities regarding how to allocate attention and resources. A distracted focus can lead to weakened support for the reform.

Central Office Support

In order to assess central office support in the cases of strong and weak matches between district context and provider expectations, we sought to develop a structure for assessing central office support across the given reforms. As readers will recognize based on earlier chapters in this volume, the five external school reforms in this study varied considerably in strategy and ambition. However, we observed they all shared a set of five functions that they expected the central office to fulfill to a greater or lesser extent. Thus, we used a set of measures for central office support that could be applied to all of the providers in this study. The particular indicators of central office support will be discussed later in this chapter.

In short, we found that central office support for the reforms' enactment and use in the study schools ranged from minimal (failing to fulfill basic contractual obligations) to extensive and comprehensive supports that exceeded provider expectations. This finding suggests that matching district context and provider expectations in terms of coupling, capacity, and alignment yielded more central office support for the reforms. We turn now to a review of the data collected on the three variables that we argue must match in order for central offices to support reform in meaningful ways.[2]

DISTRICT–PROVIDER MATCHES

Overall, the match between district context and provider expectations varied. In this section, we discuss those matches in terms of coupling, capacity, and alignment. We then discuss the implications for the presence or absence of such a match.

Coupling

The amount of central office support for the reforms was related to a combination of the level of autonomy providers expected the central offices to give and the level of autonomy the central offices traditionally had given to high schools. This also can be characterized as how "tightly coupled" the central office–high school relationship was in those districts. For the purposes of this study, the level of the central office–high school coupling was determined by the extent to which central office staff participated in the daily work of instructional improvement at the high school level. Many (although not all) of the districts in this study used standard curricula, consolidated authority over personnel decisions at the central office, and worked in partnership with schools to make decisions about how to spend at least some discretionary dollars.

The area of greatest variability across our districts was the extent to which central office staff members engaged in work around the "technical core" of teaching (Elmore, 2000). Elmore describes this core as

> detailed decisions about what should be taught at any given time, how it should be taught, what students should be expected to learn at any given time, how they should be grouped within classrooms for purposes of instruction, what they should be required to do to demonstrate their knowledge, and, perhaps most importantly, how their learning should be evaluated. (p. 5)

For the central office, supporting this core could include clear guidance about and close monitoring (more than formal annual evaluations) of instructional practices, guidance on the articulation and alignment of content and practice, participating in student placement decisions, and helping teachers to design and use appropriate assessment instruments. In cases where central offices were performing all of these tasks in partnership with their high schools, we characterized the level of coupling as "high." In districts where central offices performed some of these activities, we characterized the level as "moderate." In several districts, the central office was engaged in one or none of these activities at the high school level, and we characterized these as having a "low" level of coupling.

The level of coupling was not always a result of the capacity to support reform that existed in the central office. Central offices had very different philosophies and traditions regarding how they interacted with their high school(s). Similarly, providers had different expectations for the central office–high school relationship. Looking across the 15 districts, there was a range in how tightly coupled central offices and high schools traditionally had been and how well that matched with provider expectations. Table 6.1 provides an overview of the contexts, expectations, and matches that we found.

District coupling. In this study, the 15 districts were split among those that had a tightly coupled relationship (high), those that had a moderately

Table 6.1. Coupling match between district context and provider expectations.

School	*Level of Coupling in District*	*Level of Coupling Expected by Provider*	*Match?*
FTF1	High	High	Match
FTF2	Moderate	High	No
FTF3	Low	High	No
HSTW1	Moderate	Moderate	Match
HSTW2	Low	Moderate	No
HSTW3	High	Moderate	Exceeds
SN1	High	High	Match
SN2	Low	High	No
SN3	Moderate	High	No
RU1	Low	Low	Match
RU2	High	Low	Exceeds
RU3	Moderate	Low	Exceeds
PLN1	Moderate	Low	Exceeds
PLN2	High	Low	Exceeds
PLN3	High	Low	Exceeds

Notes: As discussed in Chapter 2, at PLN3 the reform was being used as a whole-school reform, very unlike the reform in other PLN schools. RU2 was in a similar situation with regard to its use of RU in comparison with the other RU school in this study.

coupled relationship (moderate), and those that had a very loosely coupled relationship (low). There was no attribute common among all central offices that worked in a tightly or loosely coupled fashion with their school(s). Districts in all categories varied in terms of number of students, number of schools, performance levels, locations, and other characteristics.

Central offices that had a tightly coupled relationship with their schools behaved in a variety of ways to exert their influence on the technical core. Among the 15 districts, six central offices were tightly coupled and had a tradition of active support for the work of their high schools. These central offices were closely involved in decisions about curriculum and instructional programs. In each of these schools, at least one central office staff member was a regular presence in the high school. In several cases, the bureaucratic line that often divides school staff and central office staff was almost imperceptible, with central office staff based in the high schools in order to support ongoing professional development and implementation of standards, and monitor progress. Central office staff frequently worked in the high school, and high school staff often served in some central office capacity.

Five central offices fell in the midrange in terms of their central office–high school coupling. These districts exerted some control over their high schools, but did not provide the comprehensive support and involvement of the districts described previously. During the study period, several of these midrange districts were in the midst of a transition from a system of largely autonomous high schools to one in which high schools had more oversight and were expected to take some direction from the central office.[3] For example, one of these central offices was recentralizing its authority after a number of years during which its high schools operated relatively autonomously and turned to the central office for help only when they thought they needed it. At the time of our research, the central office, having experienced staff turnover in several key leadership positions, was seeking to recentralize a number of functions and have high schools create a common curriculum, syllabi, and course exams. Another district exerted central office authority primarily to ensure compliance with new state curriculum and teaching standards. Generally speaking, these central offices focused their energies on one or two areas (for example, requiring periodic assessments and reviewing data with school staff) and would serve in other areas as an available resource when schools requested help. In one district, while the central office exerted authority over curriculum and instruction, the high school strongly resisted this authority, resulting in our assessment of moderate coupling between the district and high school.

Finally, we had four districts that had almost no central office participation in their high schools. These districts retained a loosely coupled system as a result of either resource constraints or their philosophy about the appropriate role for the central office. For example, we visited at least two districts that limited central office involvement and tried to devolve as much money as possible to empower principals at the school level to make decisions about the instructional program. This was done as part of an accountability system in which principals were responsible for performance and were given the latitude to make changes as they saw fit.

Provider expectations for coupling. The five reforms in this study also varied in the degree to which they expected the central office to assume a primary role in the technical core of high schools. Although all of the reforms were happy to work closely with central office partners at any opportunity, it was not always a requirement. As Figure 6.2 illustrates, the five reforms could be arrayed in order in terms of the level of coupling that they expected the district to embody.

Only one of the five reforms, SchoolNet (SN), expected the implementation effort to be *led* by the central office. In this case, implementation relied on active central office involvement in every aspect of implementing the reform, including building expertise about the reform at the school level, creating or selecting district-wide assessments connected to district-wide standards, and developing systems for using data to make decisions and for monitoring this use at the school level. Although SN has tools for central office staff to use to accomplish all of these things, central offices must actively use them and push schools to use them. Thus, this reform depended heavily on a very tightly coupled central office–high school relationship.

Other reforms took a greater share of the burden for working directly with schools. For example, First Things First (FTF) expected central offices to be closely attuned to and take an active role in ensuring the reform's progress. This was done in a relatively tightly coupled fashion, with instructional coaches, observation of classroom practice, and common

Figure 6.2. Range of coupling among reform systems.

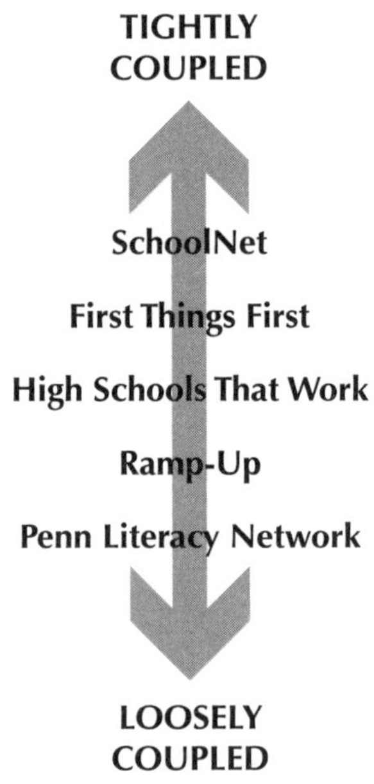

planning-time activities. While the provider expected the central office to play this role, our evidence shows that the provider itself could offer a great deal of support directly to schools, supplementing central office intervention where necessary.

Those reforms that did not depend on a tightly coupled central office–high school relationship instead relied on some degree of district flexibility in order to permit the appropriate staffing changes, student scheduling, modifications to course-taking requirements, or resource allocation adjustments needed for the reform to function in the high school. Reforms like High Schools That Work (HSTW), which do not necessarily depend on a great deal of central office involvement at the school level, needed active central office consent in order for schools to make the changes. Other reforms, like Ramp-Up (RU) and the Penn Literacy Network (PLN), required less schoolwide modification and thus could be undertaken with even less central office involvement.

Capacity

Central office support for the reform also was influenced by the fiscal and staff capacity available within the central office. As Table 6.2 shows, central office capacity in both areas varied substantially across the 15 districts and had implications for their ability to meet provider expectations of districts.

Central office capacity. The fiscal capacity of each district influenced the extent to which the central office could cover core reform costs as well as supplemental support. In general, the majority of districts had sufficient fiscal capacity to operate but ranged in their ability to assume additional large costs. The five districts with high fiscal capacity were located either in relatively affluent suburban communities or in large districts that were able to garner substantial government and private funding to meet a wide range of student needs (schools in these districts had many students who were struggling academically). The eight districts with moderate fiscal capacity generally had sufficient capacity to operate their school systems, but the prospects for assuming greater costs that were needed for additional implementation supports were constrained. Five of these districts were located in smaller suburban or rural districts and had only one or two high schools. The other three were located in medium-sized urban communities. Two districts had relatively low fiscal capacity. During the study period, one district was essentially bankrupt and still owed the provider for basic implementation costs. In another case, the district faced a budget crisis. With jobs and programs threatened, the central office was under intense pressure to limit expenditures. Finally, one district had the

Table 6.2. Capacity match between district context and provider expectations.

School	*Level of Fiscal Capacity in Central Office*	*Level of Fiscal Capacity Expected by Provider*	*Match?*	*Level of Staff Capacity in Central Office*	*Level of Staff Capacity Expected by Provider*	*Match?*	*Overall Capacity Match*
FTF1	High	High	Match	High	High	Match	Match
FTF2	Low	High	No	Moderate	High	No	No
FTF3	High	High	Match	Low	High	No	No
HSTW1	Moderate	Moderate	Match	Moderate	Moderate	Match	Match
HSTW2	Moderate	Moderate	Match	Moderate	Moderate	Match	Match
HSTW3	Moderate	Moderate	Match	High	Moderate	Exceeds	Exceeds
SN1	High	High	Match	High	High	Match	Match
SN2	Moderate	High	No	Moderate	High	No	No
SN3	Moderate	High	No	Moderate	High	No	No
RU1	Low	Low	Match	Low	Low	Match	Match
RU2	Moderate	Low	Exceeds	High	Low	Exceeds	Exceeds
RU3	Moderate	Low	Exceeds	Moderate	Low	Exceeds	Exceeds
PLN1	High	Low	Exceeds	Moderate	Low	Exceeds	Exceeds
PLN2	High	Low	Exceeds	Moderate	Low	Exceeds	Exceeds
PLN3	Moderate	Low	Exceeds	High	Low	Exceeds	Exceeds

fiscal capacity to fund the reform at the outset and even upgrade technology to support the reform, but this central office also was focused on fulfilling other large and more pressing fiscal priorities, including significant construction.

Staff capacity in the central offices can be understood in terms of the absolute number of central office staff available, as well as the knowledge and skills these individuals possessed to support high school efforts. The knowledge and skills of central office staff, particularly in the area of curriculum and instruction, varied widely. This variation was a function of both the existing expertise and the stability of the central office staff. In the 13 districts with high or moderate staff capacity, leaders in the central office possessed knowledge, skills, and experience that appeared to be commensurate with the needs of their high schools. Where individuals did not have sufficient knowledge and skills, they were able to acquire greater expertise. Limitations in terms of existing staff expertise and knowledge were most apparent in two particularly troubled and poor school districts. In both districts, the central office had limited familiarity with high school curriculum efforts underway. For example, in one district, curriculum and instruction staff had a background in elementary school curriculum but little experience with secondary school curriculum.

Provider expectations for central office capacity. The five providers held expectations that presumed a level of fiscal and staff capacity in the central office. The most basic expectation held by the providers was financial. Expectations of central office financial support ranged from several thousand dollars to millions of dollars. The providers relied primarily on the central office to fund the initiative directly or to secure the necessary funds from other sources.[4] In addition to covering the basic reform costs, the ability of the central offices to fund supplemental costs as needs arose was often pivotal in providing expected support. These supplemental funds supported additional technical assistance and materials from the provider in the form of workshops, mentoring, and site visits.

The five reforms held different expectations of staff capacity within the central office. While each reform sought a point person, the two targeted reforms (PLN and RU) relied on this person primarily for basic communication around issues of scheduling, materials procurement, or contractual arrangements. Their contact was typically infrequent. Both reforms encouraged central office interest and involvement, but neither specified clear roles or expectations for central office staff. HSTW relied to a slightly greater degree on this point person to assist with aligning reform priorities with district efforts. In contrast, both FTF and SN depended heavily on central office staff. FTF sought a full-time point person to facilitate the reform's progress within the central office, and SN worked on a sometimes daily basis with members of a project team composed of high-level central office staff to build, plan, and implement the SN system. With the exception of the technology office for SN, the five providers sought central office support primarily from the curriculum and instruction offices. Clearly, the match between provider expectations for central office support and the central office's actual capacity would have clear implications for the support that was provided. The importance of this match and the effect on various types of program support will be discussed later in the chapter.

Alignment

Although we have saved it for last, alignment is the "first among equals" in the set of three district-focused variables that we argue are essential for high-level central office support. Without aligning district priorities and practice with the reform, the central office is unlikely to devote the resources necessary to support the reform in a meaningful way. For the purposes of this analysis, we are considering alignment in two ways: (1) alignment between the reform and the district's strategies and efforts in high schools, and (2) alignment between the reform under study and other reforms present in the district. Table 6.3 summarizes our findings.

Alignment between the reform and district efforts. All district leaders felt that improving student achievement was their top priority for high schools. They had a number of metrics to assess improved achievement, including state test scores, percentages of students taking the SAT, and course completion. Several also identified intermediate steps in pursuit of improved achievement. These steps included improved attendance, de-

Table 6.3. Alignment match between district context and provider expectations.

School	*Level of Alignment Between Reform and District Efforts*	*Level of Alignment Expected by Provider*	*Match?*
FTF1	High	High	Match
FTF2	Moderate	High	No
FTF3	Low	High	No
HSTW1	Moderate	High	No
HSTW2	Moderate	High	No
HSTW3	High	High	Match
SN1	High	High	Match
SN2	Low	High	No
SN3	High	High	Match
RU1	Low	Low	Match
RU2	High	Low	Exceeds
RU3	Moderate	Low	Exceeds
PLN1	Low	Moderate	No
PLN2	Low	Moderate	No
PLN3	High	Moderate	Exceeds

creased disciplinary actions, and increased enrollment in higher level courses. In support of both interim and long-term goals, district leaders had developed particular strategies.

In some cases, central office staff saw the reform as the core approach for reaching higher achievement levels. We defined this context as a district in which the reform and district priorities were highly aligned ("high"). The reforms that were intended as whole-school (FTF and HSTW) or whole-district (SN) reforms lent themselves more easily to full alignment with district priorities. Because these reforms possessed strategies to address a number of the causes of low achievement, they frequently were viewed as being highly aligned. We should make clear that although district leaders may have viewed a reform as highly aligned with district priorities, this does not necessarily imply these leaders actively supported the reform. Of the six districts that were using a whole-school reform, two viewed the reform as serving to unify and coordinate their improvement initiatives. In these cases, the districts and the reforms had essentially indistinguishable priorities at the high school level. The other four districts using a whole-school reform had less complete alignment of priorities, although in some cases they sought to adopt elements of the whole-school reforms and made those district priorities. In these cases, the central office viewed the reforms as beneficial for the schools where partnerships had been developed, and certainly saw the reforms as supportive of and generally aligned with district priorities, but they continued to pursue goals and develop materials apart from the reform (defined as "moderate" alignment). In at least two of these cases, the central office had been instrumental in forging the partnership with the provider but did not have explicit plans for how the priorities of the reform and priorities of the district would align. As a district-wide reform, SN expected high alignment between district priorities and the reform. In two districts, there was strong evidence of this high level of alignment. In the remaining district, the reform's alignment with other reform initiatives was declining with changes in district leadership.

Districts in which schools were using more targeted reforms (PLN and RU) also varied in the extent to which they aligned district priorities with the efforts of the providers. In two cases, the central office worked in a systemic and concerted fashion to align district priorities with the reform wherever possible.[5] In both of these cases, the partnerships were forged at the central office level (as opposed to the school level). In creating the partnerships, districts planned to use certain instructional practices introduced by the reform. Using these practices influenced district decisions regarding the support strategies selected, such as classroom visit protocols, lesson-planning guides, and the choice of curriculum materials. In the other four districts that used targeted reforms, the reforms generally impacted only the teachers who had volunteered or been assigned to undergo particular training. Although district leaders clearly viewed the reforms as being helpful to teachers and/or students, they made little or no effort to align practices in instruction or curriculum in the district at large with the reform-oriented practices (defined as "low" alignment).

Alignment between the reform and other reform initiatives. In general, we can say that where district-wide priorities for high schools were aligned with the reform being studied, this alignment effort was extended to include other reform partnerships. In these cases, central office staff had a vision of the way in which each reform supported their priorities.

Across our sample, we found several districts that appeared to have made strategic choices about the selection and role of other reforms and how they aligned with the reforms that are the focus of this study. We also found districts that allowed teachers to devote time and resources to reforms that were not clearly aligned with any other initiatives. This contributes to what has been called the "Christmas tree effect" (Raphael, Gavelek, Hynd, Teale, & Shanahan, 2002), in which a particular set of teachers or a single grade level adopts an initiative or instructional approach without connecting it to the broader instructional program.

It appears that those districts that had schools working with a whole-school reform were conscious of the need to align other reforms with the whole-school reform. This sometimes was accomplished through the initiative of central office staff and sometimes resulted through intervention by a representative from the provider. Even where explicit efforts were made to align other reforms with the whole-school reform, central office staff acknowledged that this might not always have been evident to school staff. In the most loosely coupled districts (as discussed earlier), the decision about alignment among reforms was made not at the district level at all, but at the school level.

In the more targeted reforms, alignment among reforms was less consistently thought of as a problem for district leaders. In the districts where RU and PLN were used in the way in which they originally were conceived (as targeting a small number of teachers), district leaders saw the reform as one of a number of initiatives that would help them to meet particular outcome goals. They did not necessarily talk about aligning a host of reforms other than to say that they were all purchased or partnered with in order to raise student achievement (or to meet one of the intermediate goals mentioned previously). For example, RU generally was viewed as a strategy to help raise reading levels more quickly than traditional practices did. District leaders did not see it as necessary to connect RU with other reform initiatives that existed in the schools. Teachers who chose to participate in PLN were expected to use the practices they learned in the service of meeting school and district goals, but there was no explicit mention of relating those practices to other reform initiatives underway in the schools.

In the two districts (PLN3 and RU2) that had modified and expanded targeted reforms in order to use at least some elements and practices schoolwide and even district-wide, district leaders thought much more like those leaders who were using the traditional whole-school reforms. In these cases, they attempted to make connections between the reform under study and other reforms and requirements. These other reform "partners" included requirements from the state that schools and districts had to meet.

Provider expectations for alignment. Provider leaders generally expected that there would not be other reforms in the district (or at least in the schools where they were working) that would conflict with their principles, philosophies, and practices. Those offering whole-school reforms expected that the central office would, at the very least, allow participating high schools to create a set of priorities that aligned well with the expectations and requirements of both the district and the reform. In general, they desired a more conscious alignment of priorities and practices according to the guidelines of the reform. Because the district has policies of its own, and often passes along state policies that impact high schools, the central office can serve as a moderator and ensure alignment with the reform. Some of these broader reforms, like FTF or SN, helped districts to align other reforms or mandated initiatives and materials with their priorities and practices.

The targeted reforms expected that the central office would see them as offering an important service in support of a district goal. These reforms generally expected that there would not be other reforms used in the particular area that they targeted. For example, PLN expected that it would be the only literacy reform at a high school, although it did not necessarily expect alignment with reforms in other areas.

CENTRAL OFFICE SUPPORT

As we stated at the beginning of this chapter, we believe the level of support a central office provides for a reform is directly related to the match between the three district characteristics reviewed in the previous section (coupling, capacity, and alignment) and the expectations of providers in those same three areas. In this section, we review the various impacts of more and less successful matches between provider expectations and district context. First, we consider the level of central office support that was found in pairs that had a "good match" in all three areas. In these cases, we generally found central office support to be sufficient to meet provider expectations. We then look at the central office support (or lack thereof) that was found when there was a "mismatch"—meaning that districts did not have contexts that met provider expectations in terms of coupling, capacity, or alignment. In these cases, we found a variety of deficiencies in the level of central office support for the reform and that the deficiencies followed a pattern based on the area in which there was a mismatch. In this section, we use the evidence to demonstrate the importance of matching provider expectations and district context in influencing central office support for reform.

When there is a good match in these three areas, a situation in which the practices of the central office are in line with the ideal context for the reform, the central office is likely to support the reform. Rather than focusing on particular areas of central office support (e.g., curriculum and instruction or data use) as other research has done (e.g., Massell & Goertz, 2002), we describe the kinds of support that providers needed from central offices in order to enact the reform in schools. We identified five types of support that were required to some extent by all of the providers in this study. These indicators provide a description of central office support for reforms and include the following:

- *Funding.* The financial resources provided by the central office to support costs associated with the reform.
- *Structural support.* Changes to traditional school or central office practice made by the central office, such as flexibility in regulations, changes to course requirements, or other management arrangements, that were necessary for a school (or the district) to pursue practices required by the reform. Structural support does not require additional ongoing support but represents a policy choice by the central office leadership.
- *Reform-specific staff support.* Central office staff members who have developed knowledge and expertise about the reform in order to support implementation.
- *Building reform expertise at the school level.* Efforts by central office staff to build knowledge and skills related to the reform among high school staff.
- *Monitoring the reform.* Activity by central office staff (perhaps in partnership with school staff) to monitor the use of reform structures and strategies at the school.

Seven of the 15 districts in this study formed a good match with their reform providers, and we found that they met or exceeded the providers' expectations for central office support. In cases of a good match, central offices supported the reform in all five ways identified above. They provided the necessary *funding* for the reform, including both start-up costs and ongoing expenses for materials, training, and equipment. They made or allowed the necessary *structural changes* required to fully implement the reform. These structural changes included changing course requirements for students, supporting the creation of school or district-wide syllabi and assessments, altering lines of authority among staff, and/or counting new training opportunities toward professional development requirements. Although reforms had very different expectations for the level of support that was to be provided by the central office, we argue that all central offices needed to have staff members sufficiently familiar with the reform to understand how it was related to other district initiatives and to provide for sustainability in the face of turnover at the school level. In settings where district context and provider expectations were well-matched, this *reform-specific staff support* was provided. Central offices that were meeting provider expectations also had the ability to *build reform expertise at the school level*. This is clearly related to the previous function and depends on the presence of staff familiar with the reform. However, it is a more activist approach, so that central offices take a proactive stance on ensuring that there is continual growth around the reform at the school level. Finally, in cases where there is a good match between central office and provider, the central office also took a role in *monitoring* the use of the reform. In these cases, where provider expectations were low, the central office had only to make sure that the trainings were taking place. When providers held higher expectations, central offices were expected to actively monitor the reform and even include elements of the reform in teacher evaluation instruments, classroom visit protocols, and general district reports on school progress. Table 6.4 summarizes these findings for each district.

Where there was not a close match between provider expectations and district context, needed support for the reform was unlikely. Eight districts did not meet the expectations of providers for implementation support they gave to schools. The areas in which central offices failed to meet expectations depended on which of the three attributes reviewed in the previous section were not a good match between the district and the provider. We will now examine the results of a mismatch in each of the three attributes discussed previously: coupling, capacity, and alignment.

Table 6.4. District–provider matches leading to support.

	Matches Between District Context and Provider Expectations			*Whether Central Office Support Met Provider Expectations by Type of Support*					
School	*Coupling Match*	*Capacity Match*	*Alignment Match*	*Funding*	*Structural Support*	*Reform-Specific Staff Support*	*Building School Expertise*	*Monitoring*	*Overall Assessment of Central Office Support*
FTF1	Match	Match	Match	Meets	Meets	Meets	Meets	Meets	Meets
FTF2	No	No	No	No	Meets	No	No	No	No
FTF3	No	No	No	Meets	No	No	No	No	No
HSTW1	Match	Match	No	Meets	Meets	Meets	Meets	Meets	Meets
HSTW2	No	Match	No	Meets	Meets	No	No	No	No
HSTW3	Exceeds	Exceeds	Match	Meets	Meets	Exceeds	Meets	Meets	Meets
SN1	Match	Match	Match	Meets	Meets	Meets	Meets	Meets	Meets
SN2	No	No	No	Meets	No	No	No	No	No
SN3	No	No	Match	Meets	Meets	Meets	No	No	No
RU1	Match	Match	Match	Meets	Meets	No	Meets	No	No
RU2	Exceeds	Exceeds	Exceeds	Exceeds	Exceeds	Exceeds	Exceeds	Exceeds	Exceeds
RU3	Exceeds	Exceeds	Exceeds	Meets	Meets	Meets	Meets	Meets	Meets
PLN1	Exceeds	Exceeds	No	Meets	No	No	Meets	Meets	No
PLN2	Exceeds	Exceeds	No	Meets	No	No	Meets	Meets	No
PLN3	Exceeds	Exceeds	Exceeds	Exceeds	Exceeds	Exceeds	Exceeds	Exceeds	Exceeds

Coupling

In the five districts where there was not a good match between the central office and provider expectations in terms of the level of central office–high school coupling (meaning that districts were more loosely coupled than providers hoped), central offices tended to perform below provider expectations in terms of *building school-level expertise* and *monitoring* the reform. In cases where the provider relied on a tightly coupled central office–high school relationship (FTF and SN), and that was not the traditional practice in the district, there was no culture in place to allow central office staff to take an active role in building staff knowledge and skill. Similarly, central offices were not accustomed to monitoring and evaluating teacher practice with the depth and/or frequency that the reforms needed. In these schools, the central office did not have a mechanism for directing professional development at the school level. In some cases (most notably in the case of FTF), the reform was able to compensate for this deficiency by supplying additional provider staff time and increasing involvement at the school level. In other cases, the absence of central office activity left these needs unfilled.

In six cases the central office exceeded provider expectations in terms of the coupled nature of the system. Among these schools, we found two scenarios. In four of these six districts, the central office built expertise and monitored the reform in the ways that the provider hoped. This is evident in Table 6.4 by looking at HSTW3, RU3, PLN1, and PLN2. Depending on the expectations of the reforms, building expertise and engaging in monitoring may have required active involvement on the part of the central office in order to meet provider expectations. In other cases, depending on the reform, building expertise and monitoring required little involvement beyond allowing a more direct high school–provider relationship to flourish. In two of the districts (RU2 and PLN3), which were even more tightly coupled than expected by the provider, the central office far exceeded the original intent of the reform and in so doing took a traditionally targeted reform and implemented it school- and district-wide. This was done with the full cooperation and support of the provider and was possible only in a tightly coupled system.

Capacity

Capacity mismatches occurred when the central office failed to meet provider expectations for central office capacity. When the central office capacity was insufficient for the reform, the central office did not have the resources to adequately provide necessary *funding, reform-specific staff support, development of school-level expertise,* and/or ability to evaluate and *monitor* the reform. There were four districts that failed to meet provider expectations for capacity. In all four cases, the provider held high expectations of the central office. In these cases, the providers—FTF and SN—expected much of the central offices in terms of funding, staff time, knowledge, and expertise. The inability of these four districts to meet expectations was caused by a number of factors. Limitations in central office staff capacity could be explained in terms of both the number of staff available and the knowledge and skills they possessed. Insufficient knowledge and skills could be caused by staff turnover as well as the existing experiential base of staff members. Only one central office (FTF2) was unable to meet basic funding costs; however, the other three central offices were limited in their ability to provide supplemental funding once implementation was underway. This type of funding was, by definition, more difficult to anticipate yet was necessary to support the implementation process at critical junctures in at the study schools. When the central office was unable to meet provider expectations for support, either the provider, school, or an outside source filled the gap, or the gap went unfilled.

When central office capacity to support the reform exceeded provider expectations, a greater level of reform use was reported in the schools. For example, the targeted literacy reform, RU, relied very little on central office capacity to support implementation and use. However, when the central office supplied additional staff, training, monitoring, and funds, the reform appeared to thrive in the targeted classrooms and spread to other classrooms (e.g., RU2).

Alignment

Alignment posed the biggest challenge among the three areas that seemed to create an impediment for central office support when there was not a good match between provider expectations and district context. Seven of the 15 districts in this study did not meet provider expectations in terms of alignment. In particular, those central offices did not align district practices and priorities with the reform. This lack of alignment meant that the reform under study was just one of a host of district initiatives that needed support from the central office. As a result, unlike the other areas of mismatch, which created support deficiencies in relatively clear areas, mismatch in alignment could cause deficiencies in any area of central office support. In central offices that did not view the reform as playing a core role in their overall improvement agenda, available capacity was not focused on supporting the reform. Alternatively, even in those districts where system coupling would have enabled central offices to provide support for the reform, the fact that the reform was not considered central or part of an aligned set of practices and priorities meant that the focus of central office attention was elsewhere.

Alignment between the reform and broader practices in the district was most important for those reforms that sought to have an impact in multiple areas of school practice. The larger the scope of change the reform was seeking to foment, the more important high degrees of alignment became. For this reason, a mismatch between provider expectations and district context in the area of alignment in districts that were working with reforms that sought wide-ranging changes in behavior (e.g., FTF, HSTW, or SN) generally was associated with an inability on the part of the district to meet support expectations. In these reforms, lack of alignment meant that central office resources and supports (where they existed at all) were spread too thinly to be productive. In contrast, for the targeted reforms (PLN and RU), alignment with other district initiatives was a relatively limited concern.

Additionally, unlike mismatches in capacity or coupling, providers and high schools could not compensate completely for a deficiency in alignment. A gap between district alignment and the context envisioned by the provider meant that schools not only did not get the support from which they would have benefited, but also periodically received conflicting messages from their central offices about where their attention should be devoted. Schools and providers also could not make the kinds of structural changes (e.g., modifications to staffing or course requirements) that were required for some of the reforms to succeed. These changes could be made only by the central office and were made only if the central office saw the reform and its own priorities as being in close alignment.

This is not to say that schools and providers did not make an effort to address alignment issues. In cases where there was a perceived mismatch in alignment either with district priorities and practices or with other reforms (including required state initiatives), leaders of reforms that targeted broad school change often made efforts to push district leaders toward more aligned practices. We also do not want to give the impression that if district practices were aligned with provider expectations, there was necessarily active central office support of the reform. In cases of the whole-school reforms, alignment was a necessary but not sufficient element of a provider–district match. As noted previously, mismatches in capacity and coupling also could prevent a central office from providing sufficient support to a reform.

Conclusion

In the research and analysis described in this chapter, we have identified three characteristics of districts and expectations of providers that should match in order to yield necessary levels of central office support for any particular reform effort. Those three characteristics/expectations are

- The *coupled* nature of the central office–high school relationship
- The human and fiscal *capacity* of the central office
- The *alignment* that the central office is prepared or able to create with regard to the reform

We found that where any one of these three matches was missing, full central office support was unlikely to be found. Given this finding, we urge providers and school leaders to make explicit their expectations and contexts in these three areas and to consider the possibilities for a match.

In combination, these findings indicate that reform success is in large part the responsibility of the central office in terms of both considering an appropriate match for the system and the types of support that are needed. In supporting reform use in schools, central offices should consider the five essential support types we found in our research, which spanned a range of reforms. The required types of support included funding, structural changes, reform-specific staff support, effort to build reform expertise at the school level, and monitoring of the reform use at the school level.

In addition, this research argues for the importance of studying further the role that the central office plays in the use of reform. The central office is one of the layers that has the potential to influence a reform as it enters the school and district environment. This influence may occur as the result of institutional limitations, choices, or unintentional mismatches, and is evident in the types of central office support provided to schools. The mismatches that we found between central office context and provider expectations may point to very different understandings about the meaning of the reform. These mismatches generally are related to insufficient central office support for the reform as intended by the providers. One would expect that a failure to meet provider expectations would have serious implications for the use of the reform at the school level. Evaluating reform use was beyond the scope of this study but is an appropriate next step in researching the role and influence of the central office in school reform efforts.

NOTES

1. In this chapter, we use the term "central office" to refer to the administrative office of the school district. The term "district" refers to the entire unit or system of schools.

2. Data for this study were drawn from interviews with 20 central office staff members and 18 provider representatives. In addition, data also were drawn from printed materials made available by the providers. Data were triangulated based on interviews with school-level leaders at the 15 high schools in this study.

3. It is worth noting that this trend echoed the relationship between states and districts. District staff mentioned that as they felt increasingly accountable for the performance of schools in the district, they felt the need to exert more control over activities at the school level.

4. While the providers typically depended on the district to cover the basic costs of implementing and operating the reform, at least one provider also turned to other funding sources, such as foundations, to cover core expenses.

5. It should be noted that the "reform" in this case refers to the districts' adaptation of the reform. In both cases, this adaptation was done with the consent and support of the provider. However, the reforms as they are presented and sold in most cases are much narrower in focus than these districts chose to make them.

REFERENCES

Bodilly, S. J., Keltner, B. R., Purnell, S. W., Reichardt, R., & Schuyler, G. (1998). *Lessons from New American Schools' scale-up phase: Prospects for bringing designs to multiple schools.* Santa Monica, CA: RAND Corporation.

Bryk, A., & Schneider, B. (2002). *Trust in schools.* New York: Russell Sage Foundation.

Corcoran, T., & Lawrence, N. (2003). *Changing district culture and capacity: The impact of the Merck Institute for Science Education Partnership* (CPRE Research Report RR-054). Philadelphia: University of Pennsylvania, Consortium for Policy Research in Education.

Datnow, A., & Stringfield, S. (2000). Working together for reliable school reform. *Journal of Education for Students Placed at Risk, 5*(1–2), 183–204.

Desimone, L. (2002). How can comprehensive school reform models be successfully implemented? *Review of Educational Research, 72*(3), 433–479.

Elmore, R. (2000). *Building a new structure for school leadership.* Washington, DC: Albert Shanker Institute.

Firestone, W. A. (1989). Using reform: Conceptualizing district initiative. *Educational Evaluation and Policy Analysis, 11*(2), 151–164.

Glennan, T. K., Bodilly, S. J., Galegher, J., & Kerr, K. A. (2004). *Expanding the reach of education reforms: Perspectives from leaders in the scale-up of educational interventions.* Santa Monica, CA: RAND Corporation.

Gross, B., & Goertz, M. E. (Eds.). (2005). *Holding high hopes: How high schools respond to state accountability policies* (CPRE Research Report No. RR-056). Philadelphia: University of Pennsylvania, Consortium for Policy Research in Education.

Hatch, T. (1998). The differences in theory that matter in the practice of school improvement. *American Educational Research Journal, 35*(1), 3–31.

Hatch, T. (2000). What does it take to "go to scale"? Reflections on the promise and perils of comprehensive school reform. *Journal of Education for Students Placed at Risk, 5*(4), 339–354.

Kronley, R. A., & Handley, C. (2003). *Reforming relationships: School districts, external organizations, and systemic change*. Providence, RI: Brown University, Annenberg Institute for School Reform.

Massell, D., & Goertz, M. E. (2002). District strategies for building instructional capacity. In A. M. Hightower, M. S. Knapp, J. A. Marsh, & M. W. McLaughlin (Eds.), *School districts and instructional renewal* (pp. 43–60). New York: Teachers College Press.

McLaughlin, M. W., & Talbert, J. E. (2001). *Professional communities and the work of high school teaching*. Chicago: University of Chicago Press.

McLaughlin, M. W., & Talbert, J. E. (2003). *Reforming districts: How districts support school reform*. Seattle, WA: Center for the Study of Teaching and Policy.

Raphael, T. E., Gavelek, J., Hynd, C. R., Teale, W. H., & Shanahan, T. (2002). Christmas trees are great, but not as models for instructional coherence in literacy. *Illinois Reading Council Journal, 30*(3), 5–7.

Spillane, J. P., & Thompson, C. L. (1997). Reconstructing conceptions of local capacity: The local education agency's capacity for ambitious instructional reform. *Educational Evaluation and Policy Analysis, 19*(2), 185–203.

Weick, K. E. (1976). Educational organizations as loosely coupled systems. *Administrative Science Quarterly, 21*(1), 1–19.

Yonezawa, S., & Datnow, A. (1999). Supporting multiple reform designs in a culturally and linguistically diverse school district. *Journal of Education for Students Placed at Risk, 4*(1), 101–126.

CHAPTER 7

Implementation as Iterative Refraction

Jonathan A. Supovitz

MANAGING THE complexities of implementation is one of the biggest challenges that leaders of complex and ambitious reforms face in the 21st century. Part of the difficulty of understanding implementation is that the possibilities for mutation are so diverse and can be due to so many different factors. Ron Heifetz (1994) of Harvard's Kennedy School of Government makes a distinction between technical challenges and adaptive challenges. A technical challenge is a problem for which there is a known solution and the demand is on practitioners to apply that solution. An adaptive challenge is a problem for which there is no known solution. Implementation is no doubt an adaptive challenge.

Over time, our understanding of the complex nature of implementation has deepened through several stages of investigation. These were described in Chapter 1 of this volume and are summarized again here. In the late 1960s and early 1970s researchers began to examine the influence of the ambitious social programs enacted under President Lyndon Johnson's Great Society. Early views of implementation were naive, conceiving of it as a relatively straightforward technical process. The failure of high-fidelity implementation was considered to be caused by purposeful and willful acts on the part of local implementing agents (Firestone, 1989; Hjern, 1982; Lipsky, 1978). As investigations of implementation became more nuanced, researchers began to recognize its contextual and programmatic contours. These included complexity, exposure, resources, training, and supervision (Dane & Schneider, 1998; Ruiz-Primo, 2006).

Researchers also recognized that adaptations occurred during the implementation process on the part of both program developers and local sites (Berman & McLaughlin, 1976). Program developers adjusted their programs in particular sites in response to local priorities and needs, and local implementers modified the programs both intentionally and unconsciously as they used their own frames of reference to understand program intent. Berman and McLaughlin's (1978) theory of mutual adaptation seemed to capture this dual adjustment perfectly. This began a debate in the research community about whether adaptation was inevitable (Berman & McLaughlin, 1978; Dusenbury, Brannigan, Falco, & Hansen, 2003; Elmore, 1996) and even desirable (Ridgely & Jerrell, 1996).

Informed by this research tradition, we began our study of reform in American high schools expecting to see variation throughout the reform implementation process that we were studying. Our research set out to understand the underlying reasons and sources of this variation. Our work was guided by two central research questions:

1. How do the reform ideas and practices of external change agents interact with school environments and teacher attributes to change instructional and organizational practices in high schools?
2. What factors both within and outside high schools explain differing levels of understanding and enactment of programs?

Even though we expected variability and adaptation, we were surprised by the complexity, breadth, and extent to which they occurred. We observed a process in which reforms were reinterpreted repeatedly by multiple actors at multiple levels of the system at multiple points in time. In some cases, the reform programs failed to get off the ground and eventually were abandoned altogether (PLN1). In other cases, targeted reforms were so influential that they were implemented schoolwide (PLN3, RU2). In still other cases, schools adopted pieces of programs selectively (HSTW1) or adjusted program components to suit their particular needs (FTF1). As we looked more closely, we found that adjustments were made at virtually every level of the system we examined and at each time point that we collected data. The programs we set out to follow repeatedly morphed in both big and small ways that often were subtly or sometimes dramatically different from their initial shapes. At times, the product of these adjustments retained the original spirit and intent of the designs, and sometimes the adjustments were quite striking. Thus the programs that were being implemented were local renditions of the designers' intent, rather than the formal designs themselves. The implications for researchers and evaluators of the understanding that local actors implement their local rendition of a formal design are significant. This is an issue that we will return to later in this chapter.

This growing recognition of the complexity of implementation led to several overall conclusions. First, the adaptation process—whereby local actors interpret and adjust the meaning of the program—occurs at multiple levels of the system. We found adjustments at the district, school leader, department or team, and teacher levels. Second, this adaptation process occurs not just once but repeatedly—albeit in different cycles and at different magnitudes—at each of these levels. At each level, adjustments might be made at one point in time for one design component and again for a different design component or even in reconsidering the same component. Third, the sources of these repeated adjustments seemed to emanate from individual considerations, social interactions, and organizational structures and routines. Examples of individual sense making abounded in our data. Organic social interactions, evidenced through school communication patterns, were also a source of design interpretations. Additionally, decisions were influenced by organizational routines and standard processes.

These overall findings led us to consider how well our findings fit with the theory of mutual adaptation. We felt that our findings were certainly consistent with this theory and the explanations of the sources of adaptation. However, the complexity of our data was not fully represented by the theory of mutual adaptation. Thus, we have developed a refined theory of reform implementation, which we call iterative refraction.

IMPLEMENTATION AS ITERATIVE REFRACTION

To acknowledge and clarify the growing understanding of the complexity of the implementation process, we introduce the theory of *iterative refraction*. Iterative refraction is the interactive process through which reforms are adjusted repeatedly as they are introduced into and work their way through school environments. Much as light or sound waves bend and change as they pass through a medium, so reforms go through a series of modifications as they enter into, and interact with, school environments.

We have chosen the idea of refraction to represent our conceptualization of the implementation process because it best captures the idea that an external reform is likely to change repeatedly as it filters through the multiple layers of the education system, including the district, school, department or team or other school subunit, and individual teachers' classrooms (see Figure 7.1). At each of these layers, the reform is likely to be interpreted—and

Figure 7.1. The refraction process.

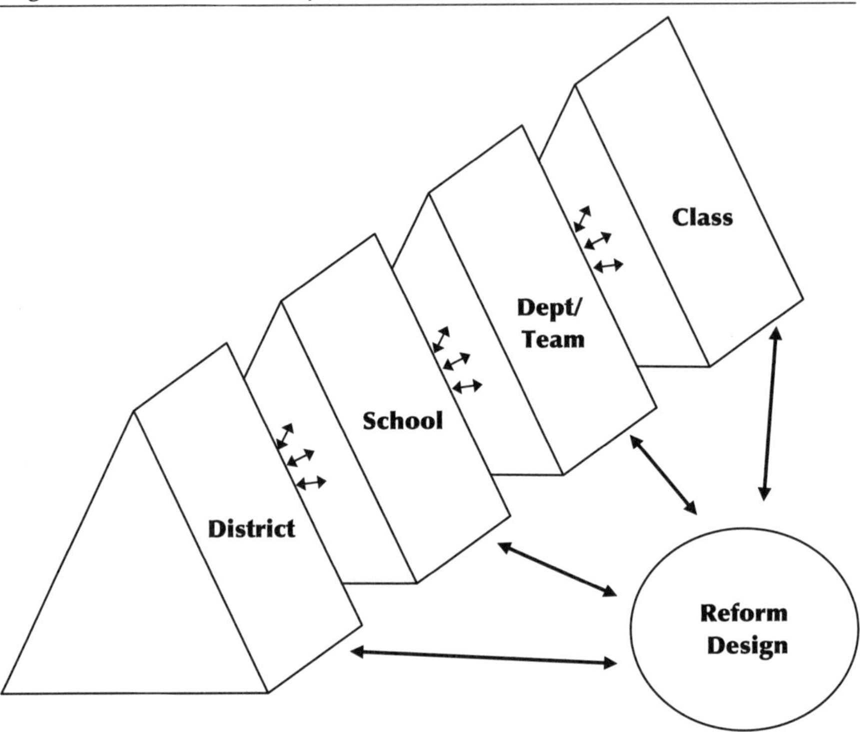

thus diffused—as it is dispersed throughout the system. The reform that begins this journey is not likely to be the reform that is enacted in the classroom. In fact, the reform may look very different in different departments within a school, and even in different classrooms within a department. Refraction perfectly captures the changes that reform goes through as it interacts with individuals and organizational conditions amid the highly interpretive processes that make up implementation.

We purposefully add the adjective *iterative* in front of refraction to represent the cyclical nature of the refraction process. We believe that refraction occurs iteratively on two independent planes. First, the iterative refraction process occurs at each level of the education system into which a reform is introduced. For example, the refraction process is occurring cyclically at the school leadership level as leaders attempt to put ideas into use in whole schools, subunits, and individual classrooms. Second, refraction iteratively occurs within each level over time, as new decisions need to be made about different components of a reform. Thus, school leaders may adjust a reform repeatedly over time as they make decisions temporally about different components of the reform.

Additionally, and importantly, the refraction process is distinct at each of these levels and points in time. First, consider differences by level. As school and district leaders take hold of reform ideas, they inevitably shape them to their needs, purposes, and goals, thus introducing one level of refraction that may depart from the original intent of reform designers. These interpreted reforms then are refracted again as they are enacted in school environments. Each of these refraction processes are distinctively different, as the actors and organizational constraints that shape the refraction process at each stage have different motivations and considerations. In high schools in particular, which are the most complex of school organizations with many distinct subcultures, the iterative refraction process is even more prismatic.

Second, consider differences over time. Even within a level there are different considerations and information at different points in time. These temporal considerations also contribute to the refraction process. The same actors—whether district administrators, school leaders, department chairs, or teachers—make multiple small and large decisions over time about how best to introduce different components of a reform. Thus the concept of iterative refraction captures the complexity of the multidimensional and multilayered implementation process. This image more closely captures what the process of reform might look like in the complex and messy reality of schools.

Our theory of iterative refraction is both a refinement of, and departure from, Berman and McLaughlin's (1978) concept of mutual adaptation, which itself has recognizable antecedents in the work of Pressman and Wildavsky (1973), who called implementation a "complex chain of reciprocal interaction" (p. xxiii). Iterative refraction is similar to its forebears in that it stresses the interactive nature of reform and school. It departs from them in that it emphasizes both the recursive nature of the interactive process and the uniqueness of each step and level in this process.

Through the iterative refraction process, the practices that end up being implemented in classrooms and schools are, in many cases, several steps removed from the original reform design. We believe that iterative refraction explains the overwhelmingly frequent research and evaluation findings that what is implemented is often a pale imitation of the originally intended reform (Bauman, Stein, & Ireys, 1991; Berman & McLaughlin, 1976; Elmore, 1996).

INSIDE ITERATIVE REFRACTION

While the theory of iterative refraction explains *how* the complex process of implementation unfolds, it provides little insight into *what influences the iterative refraction process*. What factors contribute to how reform ideas get interpreted and reinterpreted as they go through the multiple layers of the education system? What dynamics guide and bind actors' considerations as they carry out reform in their own particular contexts and situations? It is through these dynamics that we can understand what forces influence implementation.

Here we draw upon the individual, social, and organizational factors that influence the implementation process. While all information is filtered through individuals during the implementation process, we also can see in the data presented in the preceding chapters that social and organizational factors play important roles in shaping the range and limitations of individual consideration.

Thus we argue that individual, social, and organizational factors all interact to influence the iterative refraction process. This can be seen in the graphical conception of this process depicted in Figure 7.2. While everything filters through the cognitive sense-making processes of individuals—influenced by their prior knowledge, beliefs, and values—other factors have substantial influence as well. As we have identified here, both social and organizational factors channel and bind the options that individuals consider. Social factors, specifically the networks of professional and social relationships, influence the array of options that individuals consider. Additionally, organizational factors play a significant role. Organizational factors include organizational structures, routines, and standard operating procedures that are developed within systems over time.

Explanations of why these adaptations occurred, focused initially on the individual interpretations of local implementers (McLaughlin, 1987; Weatherly & Lipsky, 1977). More recent research has pushed individual response further, exploring the cognitive process of individual sense making through the implementation process (Cohen & Hill, 2001; Spillane, Reiser, & Reimer, 2002; Yanow, 1996). According to these and other authors, implementation hinges on the implementer's understanding of the reform's demands and expectations. From this perspective, sense making is influenced by schemas or mental models of how the world operates (Gentner & Stevens, 1983; Keil, 1989; Markus & Zajonc, 1995). Schemas are complex combinations of prior knowledge (Greeno, Collins, & Resnick, 1996), and values and beliefs (Mandler, 1984; Rumelhart, 1980). In their review of the literature on sense making, Spillane, Reiser, and Gomez (2006) identified three implications for reform implementation:

Figure 7.2. Factors influencing iterative refraction.

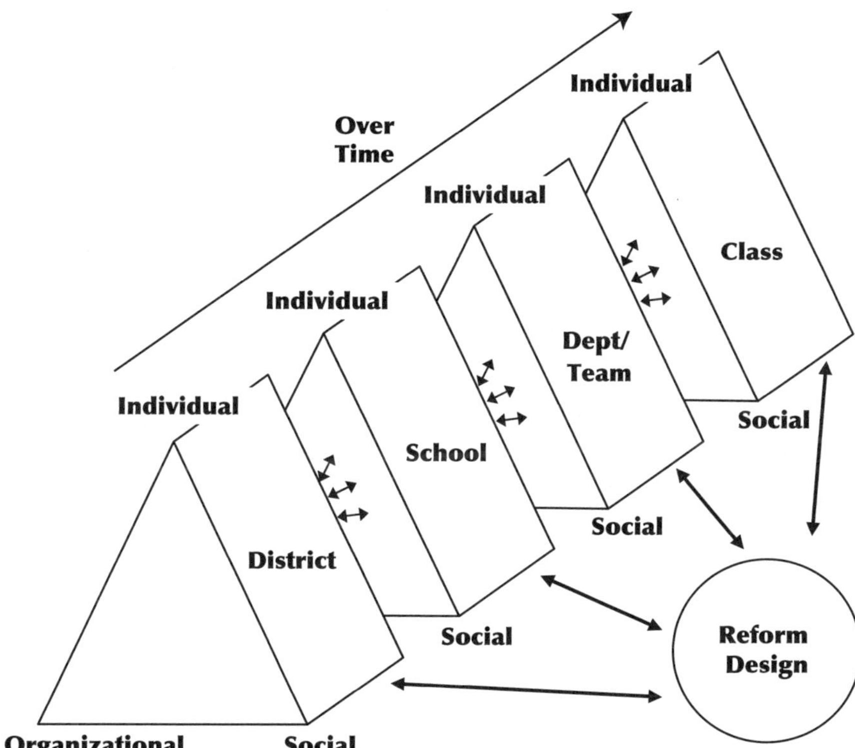

1. Individuals may have different interpretations of the same message.
2. New ideas may be misunderstood as familiar ones and interpreted to mean the same things as ideas that are already held.
3. Understanding may focus on superficial features of a reform, missing deeper relationships and contributing to misimplementation.

An abundant body of research also has described the social influences on individual cognition and action (Coburn, 2001; Coleman, 1988; Lin, 2001; Spillane et al., 2006). Social interactions define communal norms and create a system of obligation (Coleman, 1988). Professional communities in schools can establish distinctive expectations for teachers' work and relationships with students (McLaughlin & Talbert, 2001). Several authors have written on the mediating role of teacher professional communities on the implementation of reform (Coburn, 2001; Stein & Brown,

1997; Supovitz, 2002). As they interact, members of both formal and informal communities share understanding and negotiate meaning (Lave & Wenger, 1991; Wenger, 1998). Research has shown that teachers in schools with strong and shared social attributes (trust, shared responsibility, collegiality, etc.) are more likely to change their instructional practice (Lee & Smith, 1996; Louis & Marks, 1998; Newmann, King, & Youngs, 2000).

To these two explanations we add an organizational interpretation as to how reforms iteratively refract as they work their way simultaneously through a school and across time within a school. While individual sense making and social sense making have been well-documented explanations of how reforms are understood and interpreted, organizational influences on implementation have been less thoroughly investigated. Because of their regular nature, organizational structures and routines contribute to the course of action that actors take (Gersick & Hackman, 1990; Langlois & Everett, 1994; Munby, Versnel, Hutchinson, Chin, & Berg, 2003). Data from our study suggest that organizational routines, structures, and practices also contribute to explanations of why adaptations occur during the reform process.

The ways that schools are organized can have a major influence on how reforms are implemented. Organizational structures and routines have long been considered to be central conduits that facilitate and impede organizational change. Pugh, Hickson, Hinings, and Turner (1968) identified five primary dimensions of organizational structure and used them to create a taxonomy of organizational types. Their dimensions included

1. The extent of specialization, or the division of labor, within an organization
2. The extent of standardization of the basic procedures of the organization
3. The extent to which rules and procedures are formalized or codified
4. The centralization or the locus of decision-making authority within the organization
5. The configuration of roles within the organization

Pierce and Delbecq (1977) postulated a series of organizational characteristics that explained a firm's degree of innovation, many of which overlapped with those developed by Pugh and colleagues (1968). These included

- Decentralization
- Formalization or level of bureaucratization

- Stratification and intraorganizational mobility
- Organizational size, with larger organizations more innovative because of resource availability and coalition building
- Age, with older organizations more tradition-bound and less able to change

Many research studies have identified organizational factors as important influences on implementation. For example, Barley (1986) examined how the introduction of a new technology into a hospital occasioned changes in organizational structures through the altering of institutionalized roles and patterns of interaction. McLaughlin and Talbert (1993) noted that implementers' work in schools is nested in multiple organizational contexts simultaneously.

Organizational routines are a particular type organizational structure that can have an influence on reform implementation. Winter (1964) defined a routine as a "pattern of behavior that is followed repeatedly, but is subject to change if conditions change" (p. 263). Cohen and Bacdayan (1994) define organizational routines as "patterned sequences of learned behavior involving multiple actors who are linked by relations of communication and/or authority" (p. 555). Routines are seen as collective organizational actions, as distinct from individual habits (Pentland & Reuter, 1994; Weick, 1990). They store organizational experience in a form that allows the organization to rapidly transfer experience to new situations. Routines provide stability (Coombs & Metcalfe, 2000; Hodgson, 1993). However, routines can be destructive when an organization's experience is transferred to inappropriate situations (Cohen & Bacdayan, 1994). Routines are a process, a "sequence of interactions" (Becker, 2004, p. 649) that occupy the "crucial nexus between structure and action" (Pentland & Reuter, 1994, p. 484). In uncertain situations actors may turn to routines readily (Becker, 2004). Routines also store organizational knowledge and therefore become a repository for organizational history and expertise (Levitt & March, 1988; Nelson & Winter, 1982). Organizational routines can be both a means for reforms to progress and the object of reforms themselves.

In sum, our theory of iterative refraction holds that individual, social, and organizational considerations work together to influence the way that reforms get interpreted and implemented as they pass through the complex organizations that are schools and school systems. Individual cognitive considerations play a central role as individuals interpret reforms through the schemata of their backgrounds, beliefs, and prior knowledge. As schools are also complex social systems with multiple levels and forms of social communities, members' resulting social interactions further shape individuals' understandings of reform purpose and intent. Finally, organizational structures and routines also play important roles in the considerations that individuals give to reforms, as they form boundaries for consideration and mediate the actions that individuals consider. High schools, with departments or teams often operating fairly autonomously from oversight and independently of one another, provide particularly fertile ground for refraction to occur.

ITERATIVE REFRACTION IN HIGH SCHOOLS

There are several tangible examples of refraction that the reader may recall from our research described in the preceding chapters. Reviewing some of these examples may help to illuminate our theory.

Individual Refraction of Reform

As Riggan and Supovitz demonstrate in Chapter 5, formal leaders in schools can play a strong role in refracting the reform design. As the authors report, in four of the eight early-implementing schools for which we have longitudinal data, school leaders "chose to modify or selectively implement design components or practices." This was done consciously as leaders decided to emphasize elements of reforms that they believed best matched the needs of their schools, or modified elements of reform programs in order to better suit the school context. As Riggan and Supovitz point out, school leaders also refracted reforms individually in an unconscious fashion, in cases where they did not personify leadership styles envisioned by the reforms or were not able to provide the types of instructional leadership that was required of them.

Individual teachers also modified reform as they enacted it in their classrooms. Chapter 2 of this volume contains several examples of this type of individual-level modification. For example, as Mueller and Hovde describe in their summary of the Penn Literacy Network, individual teachers "tended to incorporate PLN strategies that aligned with their existing practice, while downplaying strategies that significantly challenged or altered it." In this way, whether consciously or unconsciously, teachers were choosing which streams of the reform reached into their classrooms and which ones were never or rarely used. Similarly, as the authors describe in Chapter 2, in their work with High Schools That Work, "most teachers selectively added to their repertoire specific practices that they found useful or effective with their students."

Providers too have to make ongoing decisions about how to respond to what Shiffman and colleagues refer to in Chapter 3 as "adjustment pressures." Several of the preceding chapters discuss the important role of the provider liaisons in guiding the use of reform at the school and district levels. Clearly, the on-the-spot decisions that liaisons must make in a wide variety of contexts occasionally emphasize various elements of a reform at any given point in time. As the authors illustrate in Chapter 3, "at times, central design principles were in conflict with one another." Provider representatives were then in the position of negotiating these conflicts in an effort to preserve the driving forces behind the reforms.

Social Relationships Refracting Reform

The relationships among individuals within the schools' communities also had implications for the refraction of reform. As Weinbaum and colleagues discuss in Chapter 4, friendship relationships played a large and significant role in influencing whom individuals in schools talked to most about their professional concerns. This influence extended to whom staff members sought out for guidance and information about the reform being introduced. The highlighting of these information pathways suggests that peer networks are a fertile source of information about reform. The knowledge base and practice being communicated in these relationships will have a profound influence on the degree to which reform ideas are put into practice. The authors of this chapter go further and suggest that teachers who were more connected to their peers through communication about the reform were more likely to report that they were using more of the practices encouraged by the reform. While we know that reform implementation is variable within schools, this finding shows how informal networks among teachers are a predictor of this implementation variability and hints at some of the social ways that reforms can be refracted at the teacher level.

This contention is further supported in Chapter 5 by Riggan and Supovitz. In that chapter we saw how social networks connected to informal leaders. The authors discuss how organically developed bonds with faculty members who hold no official leadership title or responsibilities serve as connective tissue for ideas to spread through a school. As a result of these connections, informal leaders possess a great deal of influence, which they use to support or oppose the design or particular elements of the design. As the authors describe, informal leaders, due to the social networks to which they are central, have the power to modify the use of an external reform program or influence how components of the reform are understood and enacted.

Even those reforms that are not necessarily meant to spread throughout a school can be modified due to social forces in the school. As we saw in Chapter 2, teachers in schools that had partnered with Ramp-Up often received information through school colleagues. As a result, their understanding of the program specifics varied, and in some cases non-Ramp-Up teachers introduced strategies or practices of the program in their own classes. This illustrates how social interactions facilitate the spread of particular elements of a reform, even if that was not necessarily the intent of the school and reform leaders. In these ways, reform designs can be refracted through the social medium of the school.

Organizational Characteristics Refracting Reform

In addition to the refraction that occurs as a result of individual action and social connections in the school, we have seen that reform is refracted as a result of organizational structures, routines, and processes. Evidence of such organizational refraction can be seen in Chapter 6, where Weinbaum and colleagues discuss how the traditional routines of the relationship between the school and central office impacted program implementation. District coupling influenced the ability of central offices to support or focus school attention on particular aspects of the reform. As the authors discuss, in some of the sites the district had a tradition of loose coupling in its relationship with high schools. Therefore, they did not engage in the level of program monitoring that the reforms expected nor were they able to support the development of school-level expertise. As a result of this loosely coupled relationship, local school actors had the latitude to favor and prioritize certain elements of the reform. In contrast, in districts where the traditional relationship between district administrators and school leaders was more tightly coupled, reforms received more attention.

We also saw how organizational features of the schools influenced reforms. Reforms like First Things First, which rely particularly heavily on changing the structures and routines of the school through such components as small learning communities, block scheduling, and the family advocacy system (FAS), are particularly susceptible to organizational refraction. We saw this in several of the sites. For example, in FTF2, organizational routines and scheduling constraints often preempted FAS meetings. In both FTF1 and FTF2, there was dissatisfaction with the FAS. In the case of FTF1 this led to several modifications, which changed the collaborative intent of the intervention and moved it back to the more familiar counselor/parent structure.

Reforms similarly can introduce changes in organizational structures and work patterns. By doing so, they may reset the patterns and routines by which people in an organization have the opportunities and occasions to interact and share knowledge with one another. For example, HSTW introduced focus teams—groups of teachers and staff organized around particular areas of work—to high schools. As another example, consider FTF, a reform that requires all the teachers who teach the same students to meet and discuss student work. By introducing a new routine into the organization, the reform changed the patterns and opportunities for professional interaction. However, in some schools, like FTF2, some team members could not attend the team meetings because of other commitments due to the scheduling constraints of the school. In this case the intent of the reform was altered as not all team members had the opportunity to share information about student skill levels and progress.

Structural constraints at the school level also caused schools to modify the reforms. For example, in one of the schools utilizing the Ramp-Up program, the small number of trained staff made it impossible for students to work with a Ramp-Up teacher for two years, as the program calls for in certain cases. Instead, this school put all students in a traditional grade-level English class after one year of Ramp-Up. As a result, the school was implementing only certain pieces of the whole Ramp-Up program. For one year, the students had the complete in-class experience. However, organizational issues prevented them from reaping the full benefit of the program as the designers intended.

In sum, the chapters in this volume are full of examples of refraction that result from individual, social, and organizational attributes present in schools and school districts. This theoretical framework provides a new way to understand the variability that has been documented in program implementation. In addition to contributing to the development of a new theoretical framework, the research in the preceding chapters also has some very real implications for a variety of audiences. We now turn our attention to the implications of this research.

IMPLICATIONS

Upon reflection, it is perhaps not surprising that a close examination of the introduction of sophisticated instructional reforms into complex high school organizations is a complicated process. Iterative refraction occurs at multiple levels across the system, driven by individual, social, and organizational factors. Given this complex and multilevel set of interactions, what implications might reform designers, district leaders, school leaders, and researchers draw from our research? The volume concludes by discussing implications for these constituencies.

Implications for Reform Designers

Although we have spent much of this volume describing the variability that can be expected in implementation, it is also true that the research described here illustrates that reform program designers have a great deal of power over the implementation of their programs. Clearly, all of the inherent school and district factors that cause refraction of reforms are beyond the control of designers. However, in Chapter 3, Shiffman and colleagues' analysis provides a wealth of information about decisions that designers can make in order to maximize capacity and support for their reform as they envision it. The findings point to four particular areas in which designers hold, to some extent, the program's fate in their hands. Program designers need to attend carefully to what they choose to emphasize, the level of complexity of the changes they are expecting, the way they engage the teachers and administrators expected to enact the program, and the ongoing implementation support.

One of our most provocative findings suggests that program designers should position high-priority elements of the reform early in the roll-out process. Even recognizing the amount of time that a reform has been in a school, it appears that the elements that are introduced early on get the most attention and support. It appears that reforms have a honeymoon period too. As other distractions and demands come to a school, it is possible that the reformer's message will be drowned out. The advice then is this: Reformers should identify the essential elements early on in the relationship with a school when they have attention, sufficient funding, and support from leadership.

Additionally, our research recommends that designers be as specific as possible in their directions to schools. In cases where particular tasks can be identified that will further the philosophies of the reforms, greater specificity will reduce the variation and interpretation. Providing schools with broad guidelines and general principles invites a great deal of local interpretation, some of which likely will be, as we have observed, in direct contradiction to the reform principles.

Some of the important and specific steps that a reform design asks a school to undertake may be quite technically complex. Schools partner with outside organizations because they or their districts recognize the need for change. However, the more complex a particular behavioral modification is going to be (whether it is in terms of changes in organization, instruction, or data analysis), the more teachers and administrators will need ongoing support in order to implement the program in a way that is consistent with the vision of the reform organization. Specificity is not sufficient in complex tasks. Teachers and administrators will need guidance about how to use even the most specific instructions in their own context. Without this guidance and support, particularly complex elements of reforms will be modified (sometimes beyond recognition) or even ignored. Furthermore, the support provided by reform organizations is most effective when it comes directly from organization staff well versed in the reform's theories and practices. Although the benefits of train-the-trainer models are understandable, this research points to the better understanding and level of commitment that is gained through direct school–provider contact.

The implementation process is rarely smooth sailing, and our work suggests that the prevailing networks of professional and social relationships have substantial influence on how reform ideas are buffeted as they enter into school environments. This suggests the importance to providers of understanding more about the existing networks of professional and social relationships that influence implementation in schools. As reforms enter into schools, they either carve out their own channels for introducing their ideas (via new structures like small learning communities or teacher teams) or rely on existing structures and channels. In either case, the mechanisms that providers choose for introducing their ideas, and the ways in which those mechanisms are connected to other networks, seem to be critical to the likelihood of success. The networks in schools are more than just contextual factors of implementation; they are the very means by which ideas spread in schools. It would behoove providers to spend more time and resources understanding the social and organizational patterns within the schools with which they intend to work.

Finally, our research suggests that reform designers should be more discerning in selecting partners, focusing their partnerships on schools and districts that have the potential to take reforms seriously. In Chapter 6, Weinbaum and colleagues demonstrate how a good match between reform organizations' expectations and the norms, traditions, and capacities of districts is much more likely to yield sufficient support for a reform than situations in which there is not a good match. By making the expectations for the central office role in reform explicit at the outset, reform organizations are much more likely to find central offices supporting their schools in ways that will enhance the presence of the reform. Another consideration in selecting partners: Reform organizations should partner with schools and districts that see the reform as a potential solution to a clearly defined, agreed-upon problem. Engagement of the enactors is increased when they sense that the reform upon which they must embark matches well with the problems that they have defined. Related to this, reform designers would do well to include in their designs opportunities for teachers and administrators to see the positive effects of the design, both in other schools that had similar challenges as well as in their own school. Attention to the engagement of staff in these ways will serve reformers well in their desire to see their program used in ways that are aligned with their original vision.

Implications for District Leaders

District leaders clearly have an essential role to play in identifying appropriate reform partners for their schools. As was alluded to above in the discussion of implications for reform program designers, district leaders need to choose their reform partners carefully if they are seeking program use that resembles the program design and theory. Based on the research by Weinbaum and colleagues in Chapter 6, it would serve district leaders well to make an honest assessment of their district prior to developing a partnership with a reform organization. Among the questions that they should ask themselves are the following:

1. *Does the relationship between my central office staff and my high school staff match well with the expectations of the reform organization?* Without the appropriate relationship, it is unlikely that central offices will be able to either monitor the reform or support school-level expertise in ways that are consonant with the reformer's expectations.
2. *Does my central office possess the physical and human resources that will be necessary to support the reform?* Reform efforts vary greatly with regard to the extent of demand they place on the central office. As we see in this volume, some depend heavily on the central office for everything from major technology support to developing a professional development strategy for the use of new tools. Others have less major demands on the central office. Regardless, central office leaders must be prepared to marshal resources in support of the reform. Where they cannot marshal the resources expected by the provider, they will have little sway over the use of the reform at the school level.
3. *Are the priorities and practices in my district well aligned with the reform program?* In order to support reform program use at the school level, district leaders need to send a clear message to actors at all levels of the system that the reform represents a serious focus of atten-

> tion for the district. We saw districts where a literacy reform was one of many being allowed to work in the district. In cases like this, actors were much less likely to devote the required time, attention, and resources to the particular reform program.

District leaders should seriously consider examining the three questions above independently and in partnership with prospective reform partners. Our research shows that the match between the answers of the two parties will be highly influential in determining the type of program implementation that may be found at the school level.

Implications for School Leaders

Formal school leaders—those that Riggan and Supovitz call "traditional-formal leaders" in Chapter 5—have a huge influence on reform implementation. Regardless of their explicit centrality to the reform efforts, and most reforms do identify a central role for formal school leaders, their advocacy plays a huge role in setting the context and establishing the agenda for reform. Without the weight and legitimacy of their support, reforms often crumble from lack of priority and inattention. Through their attention, formal leaders create pressure for faculty to implement reforms and thereby create social expectations and provide tacit incentives for faculty members to implement the called-for changes.

As they implement reforms, formal school leaders also need to recognize, and capitalize on, the influence on their faculties of informal leaders. Our research in the area of leadership revealed that there are many instructional leaders in schools who do not hold formal leadership titles, yet are very influential to their peers. These informal leaders can support or oppose reforms, yet regardless have inordinate influence on the opinions of their colleagues. Further, informal leaders can provide a unique type of reform support to peers who are grappling with the fine-grained details of reform implementation. They share the implementation experience and thus have increased credibility as well as the trust of their comrades. School leaders can capitalize on the informal leaders who are arrayed in virtually every school. It is not necessary to thrust these people into provider-formal or other titled positions; in fact, part of the influence of informal leaders grows out of their unofficial status. Rather, school leaders can identify informal leaders, assess their attitudes toward the reforms of interest, and depending on the assessment either subtly isolate them or place them in situations where they can maximally provide valuable support to colleagues.

Implications for Researchers

For researchers, the findings of this study speak more to complex reforms that are intended to be implemented across one or a series of high schools rather than to smaller, more targeted reforms that have a narrower scope. As the findings in Chapter 3 of this volume indicate, and many researchers also have noted (Dane & Schneider, 1998; Mowbray, Holter, Teague, & Bybee, 2003; Ruiz-Primo, 2006), programs with broader and more ambitious scopes are more likely to be adjusted during the implementation process. In some cases this may be simply because more complex designs have more components to be managed by local sites. Or it could be because there are more opportunities for local leaders and teachers to reinterpret the intentions of complex reforms. Our theory of iterative refraction attempts to identify both the levels and sources of these interpretations.

The data from this study, as well as the theory of iterative refraction, can help researchers as they try to understand the processes that reforms go through as they wend their way through local sites. What is clear both from our work and that of others is that replicable complex reforms are very difficult to create. Rather than resisting the seemingly inevitable iterative refractions, what we can hope to do is to better understand how reforms are changed as they enter into the dynamic cultures and environments of schools and school systems, and better predict the implications of these adjustments.

If we understand the degree of resilience in reforms as they go through the implementation process, then we will be better able to hold constant those things that are integral, while allowing, and even encouraging, adjustments in those things that are not essential to the reform but may be very important for local sites to retain control over. The contested terrain here is to what extent adjustments can be tolerated without changing the reform's essential intent. Ruiz-Primo's (2006) concept of the "degree of deviation" is useful here to distinguish the extent to which implementers can deviate and still achieve the program's goals.

Despite the findings of this study, which show that refraction occurs frequently and at multiple levels of the system, this does not say that replicable reforms are impossible to attain. In fact, the variability that we saw in this study of five reform programs being implemented in 15 high schools speaks to the importance of educational researchers and evaluators better understanding the source of implementation variation and distinguishing between constructive and destructive variability. In some cases changes in a design at the local level actually result in productive activity, whereas in other cases changes dilute the intent of the reform (Blakely et al., 1987).

Several promising research strategies would appear to help in these situations. First, researchers and evaluators should take a more holistic approach to studying reforms (Supovitz & Taylor, 2005), encompassing the entire process and treating deviations as potentially useful innovations rather than limitations. Second, theory-based evaluation approaches (see Gottfredson, 1984; Weiss, 1997) would help researchers and evaluators to distinguish between refractions that change the theory of a reform from those that may change the particularities of a reform but are really consistent with its philosophy. This strategy presumes, of course, that the power of the reform comes from its theory of improvement, and that the chief consideration of the researcher is to address whether or not adjustments conform to the underlying theory.

In today's educational research environment, researchers are being exhorted to enact the highest quality research studies. The stated "gold standard" has become experiments of programs randomly assigned to students, schools, or districts. These studies are thought to provide definitive evidence of the effectiveness of educational interventions—to show what works and what doesn't. However, such studies often leave unanswered the more important question of *why* things do or do not work. As a field, we might start to think of an even higher standard for educational research. The "platinum standard" for experimental studies could incorporate implementation metrics that explicate more precisely where and how reforms refract as they go through the implementation process. With platinum standard research, we would know not only what works, but how and why.

REFERENCES

Barley, S. (1986). Technology as an occasion for structuring: Evidence from observations of CT scanners and the social order of radiology departments. *Administrative Science Quarterly, 31*(1), 78–108.

Bauman, L. J., Stein, R. E. K., & Ireys, H. T. (1991). Reinventing fidelity: The transfer of social technology among settings. *American Journal of Community Psychology, 19*, 619–639.

Becker, M. (2004). Organizational routines: A review of the literature. *Industrial and Corporate Change, 13*(4), 643–677.

Berman, P.,& McLaughlin, M. W. (1976). Implementation of educational innovation. *The Educational Forum, 40*, 345–370.

Berman, P., & McLaughlin, M. W. (1978). *Federal programs supporting educational change: Vol. VIII. Implementing and sustaining innovations.* Santa Monica, CA: RAND Corporation.

Blakely, C. H., Mayer, J. P., Gottschalk, R. G., Schmitt, N., Davidson, W., Roitman, D. B., & Emshoff, J. G. (1987). The fidelity–adaptation debate: implications for the implementation of public sector social programs. *American Journal of Community Psychology, 15*, 253–268.

Coburn, C. E. (2001). Collective sensemaking about reading: How teachers mediate reading policy in their professional communities. *Educational Evaluation and Policy Analysis, 23*(2), 145–170.

Cohen, D. K., & Hill, H. C. (2001). *Learning policy: When state education reform works.* New Haven, CT: Yale University Press.

Cohen, M.D., & Bacdayan, P. (1994). Organizational routines are stored as procedural memory: Evidence from a laboratory study. *Organization Science, 5*(4), 554–568.

Coleman, J. S. (1988). Social capital in the creation of human capital. *American Journal of Sociology, 94*, S95–S120.

Coombs, R.,& Metcalfe, S. (2000). Organizing for innovation: Co-ordinating distributed innovation capabilities. In N. Foss & V. Mahnke (Eds.), *Competence, governance, and entrepreneurship—advances in economic strategy research* (pp. 209–231). Oxford: Oxford University Press.

Dane, A. V., & Schneider, B. H. (1998). Program integrity in primary and early secondary prevention: Are implementation effects out of control? *Clinical Psychology Review, 18*, 23–45.

Dusenbury, L., Brannigan, R., Falco, M., & Hansen, W. B. (2003). A review of research on fidelity of implementation: Implications for drug abuse prevention in school settings. *Health Education Research, 18*(2), 237–256.

Elmore, R. F. (1996). Getting to scale with good educational practice. *Harvard Educational Review, 66*(1), 1–26.

Firestone, W. A. (1989). Using reform: Conceptualizing district initiative. *Educational Evaluation and Policy Analysis, 11*(2), 151–164.

Gentner, D., & Stevens, A. L. (Eds.). (1983). *Mental models*. Hillsdale, NJ: Erlbaum.

Gersick, C. J., & Hackman, J. R. (1990). Habitual routines in task-performing groups. *Organisational Behaviour and Human Decision Processes, 47*, 65–97.

Gottfredson, G. D. (1984). A theory-ridden approach to program evaluation. *American Psychologist, 39*(10), 1101–1112.

Greeno, J., Collins, A., & Resnick, L. B. (1996). Cognition and learning. In R. Calfee & D. Berliner (Eds.), *Handbook of educational psychology* (pp. 15–46). New York: Macmillan.

Heifetz, R. A. (1994). *Leadership without easy answers.* Cambridge, MA: Belknap Press.

Hjern, B. (1982). Implementation research: The link gone missing. *Journal of Public Policy, 2*, 301–308.

Hodgson, G. M. (1993). *Economics and evolution.* Cambridge: Polity Press.

Keil, F. C. (1989). *Concepts, kinds and cognitive development.* Cambridge, MA: MIT Press.

Langlois, R. N., & Everett M. (1994). What is evolutionary economics? In L. Magnusson (Ed.), *Evolutionary and neo-Schumpeterian approaches to economics* (pp. 11–48). Dordrecht, the Netherlands: Kluwer.

Lave, J., & Wenger, E. (1991). *Situated learning: Legitimate peripheral participation.* Cambridge: Cambridge University Press.

Lee, V. E., & Smith, J. B. (1996). Collective responsibility for learning and its effects on gains in achievement for early secondary school students. *American Journal of Education, 104*(2), 103–147.

Levitt, B., & March, J. (1988). Organizational learning. *Annual Review of Sociology, 14*, 319–340.

Lin, N. (2001). *Social capital: A theory of social structure and action.* Cambridge, England: Cambridge University Press.

Lipsky, M. (1978). Standing the study of public policy implementation on its head. In W. D. Burnham & M. W. Weinberg (Eds.), *American politics and public policy* (pp. 391–402). Cambridge, MA: MIT Press.

Louis, K. S., & Marks, H. M. (1998). Does professional community affect the classroom? Teachers' work and students' experiences with school restructuring. *American Journal of Education, 106*(4), 532–575.

Mandler, J. M. (1984). *Stories, scripts, and scenes: Aspects of schema theory.* Hillsdale, NJ: Erlbaum.

Markus, H., & Zajonc, R. B. (1985). The cognitive perspective on social psychology. In G. Lindzey & E. Aronson (Eds.), *Handbook of social psychology* (pp. 137–230). New York: Random House.

McLaughlin, M. W. (1987). Learning from experience: Lessons from policy implementation. *Educational Evaluation and Policy Analysis, 9*(2), 171–178.

McLaughlin, M. W., & Talbert, J. E. (1993). *Contexts that matter for teaching and learning.* Stanford: Center for Research on the Context of Secondary School Teaching.

McLaughlin, M. W., & Talbert, J. E. (2001). *Professional communities and the work of high school teaching.* Chicago: University of Chicago Press.

Mowbray, C., Holter, M. C., Teague, G. B., & Bybee, D. (2003). Fidelity criteria: Development, measurement, and validation. *American Journal of Evaluation, 24*(3), 315–340.

Munby, H., Versnel, J., Hutchinson, N. L., Chin, P., & Berg, D. H. (2003). Workplace learning and the metacognitive functions of routines. *Journal of Workplace Learning, 15*, 94–104.

Nelson, R. R., & Winter, S. G. (1982). *An evolutionary theory of economic change.* Cambridge, MA: Harvard University Press.

Newmann, F. M., King, B., & Youngs, P. (2000). Professional development that addresses school capacity: Lessons from urban elementary schools. *American Journal of Education, 108*(4), 259–299.

Pentland, B. T., & Reuter, H. H. (1994). Organizational routines as grammars of action. *Administrative Science Quarterly, 39*(3), 484–510.

Pierce, J. L., & Delbecq, A. L. (1977). Organization structure, individual attitudes and innovation. *The Academy of Management Review, 2*(1), 27–37.

Pressman, J. L., & Wildavsky, A. B. (1973). *Implementation: How great expectations in Washington are dashed in Oakland.* Berkeley: University of California Press.

Pugh, D. S., Hickson, D. J., Hinings, C. R., & Turner, C. (1968). Dimensions of organization structure. *Administrative Science Quarterly, 13*(1), 65–105.

Ridgely, M. S., & Jerrell, J. M. (1996). Analysis of three interventions for substance abuse treatment of severely mentally ill people. *Community Mental Health Journal, 32*, 561–572.

Rumelhart, D. E. (1980). Schemata: The building blocks of cognition. In R. Spiro, B. Bruce, & W. Brewer (Eds.), *Theoretical issues in reading comprehension* (pp. 33–58). Hillsdale, NJ: Erlbaum.

Ruiz-Primo, M.A. (2006). A multi-method and multi-source approach for studying fidelity of implementation (CSE Report 677). National Center for Research on Evaluation, Standards, and Student Testing. Los Angeles: Author.

Spillane, J. P., Reiser, B. J., & Gomez, L. (2006). Policy implementation and cognition: The role of human, social, & distributed cognition in framing policy implementation. In M. Honig (Ed.), *New directions in educational policy implementation: Confronting complexity* (pp. 47–64). Albany: State University of New York Press.

Spillane, J. P., Reiser, B. J., & Reimer, T. (2002). Policy implementation and cognition: Reframing and refocusing implementation research. *Review of Educational Research, 72*(3), 387–431.

Stein, M. K., & Brown, C. (1997). Teacher learning in a social context: Integrating collaborative and institutional processes with the study of teacher change. In E. Fennema & B. S. Nelson (Eds.), *Mathematics teachers in transition* (pp. 155–191). Mahwah, NJ: Erlbaum.

Supovitz, J. A. (2002). Developing communities of practice. *Teachers College Record, 104*(8), 1591–1626.

Supovitz, J. A., & Taylor, B. S. (2005). Systemic education evaluation. *American Journal of Evaluation, 26*(2), 204–230.

Weatherly, R., & Lipsky, M. (1977). Street-level bureaucrats and institutional innovation: Implementing special-education reform. *Harvard Educational Review, 47*(2), 171–197.

Weick, K. E. (1990). The vulnerable system: An analysis of the Tenerife air disaster. *Journal of Management, 16*, 571–593.

Weiss, C. H. (1997). Theory-based evaluation: Past, present, and future. *New Directions for Evaluation, 76*, 4–56.

Wenger, E. (1998). Communities of practice: Learning, meaning and identity. Cambridge: Cambridge University Press.

Winter, S. G. (1964). Economic "natural selection" and the theory of the firm. *Yale Economic Essays, 4*, 225–272.

Yanow, D. (1996). *How does a policy mean? Interpreting policy and organizational actions*. Washington, DC: Georgetown University Press.

 APPENDIX

Research Design

THIS TWO-YEAR longitudinal study focused primarily on high schools in the early stages of their implementation of a set of school improvement efforts designed by organizations external to the school and district. In particular, we focused on three types of school improvement programs: whole-school reform programs, interventions targeted to improve literacy, and reforms intended to assist schools and teachers with analyzing student performance data as a means of guiding instruction.

Our emphasis on these three reform types grew out of findings from a prior phase of CPRE's Study of High School Strategies for Instructional Improvement. Between 2002 and 2004, we conducted a study of 48 low-performing high schools' efforts to respond to state accountability pressure. In that study we investigated a stratified random sample of low-performing high schools' efforts to improve their performance. Among the major findings of that study was that whole-school reform programs, programs to improve state reading and writing performance, and data use strategies were three of the major efforts that high schools chose in efforts to improve their performance. Informed by these findings, we chose these categories of interventions to guide this research.

Beginning in the spring of 2004, we began to collect data on numerous interventions that fell into the three categories of literacy, data use, and whole-school reform. We sought out programs that intended to have a significant impact on instructional practices at the high school level and on which some promising evidence was available. In the summer of 2004, we selected six programs, two in each category, and secured agreements of participation with program leaders. The programs that we identified were: First Things First (FTF) and High Schools That Work (HSTW) as the whole-school reform programs; the Penn Literacy Network (PLN) and Ramp-Up to Literacy (RU) as the literacy reform programs; and SchoolNet

(SN) as the data use program. Another data use program initially agreed to participate but then declined once the study was underway. At that point in the study, it was too late to recruit a replacement program.

In the summer of 2004 we asked each of the participating program providers to nominate three schools with which they were working to participate in the study. Two of the schools were to be at early stages of the reform adoption process, one just beginning a relationship with the program and the other just beginning its second year. We also asked each provider to nominate a third school that was in its third to fifth year of work with the program and represented a "best case scenario" from the perspective of reform leaders. This was an explicitly purposive sampling strategy. Providers had the opportunity to identify both early- and fully implementing sites. Using this sample, we had the opportunity to watch how implementation unfolded in sites at both earlier and later stages of work with each program.

SAMPLE

As described above, 15 schools were selected by the reform organizations for us to visit. There were several instances in which schools declined to participate in this research. In these cases, we went back to the provider for alternative nominations. The resulting sample represented a very diverse set of American high schools. Table A.1 shows selected characteristics of the final sample of high schools in the study. These schools were located in 10 states around the country. Two of the 15 high schools were in rural areas, two in mid-sized cities, seven in urban fringe areas, and four in urban areas. The sample averaged 44% students receiving free or reduced-price lunch, with a standard deviation of 34%. On average, the schools were 43% students of color, but this varied widely. Five of the schools were 90% or more White, while three of the schools were 90% or more students of color. The sample ranged in school size from a small 400-student high school in Mississippi to a Texas school with two campuses and almost 4,800 students. The average school size in the sample was just over 1,400 students. Finally, the sample ranged in terms of student performance on standardized tests. In three of the schools, under 15% of students were performing at standard on their state reading assessments, while in five of the schools, over 80% of students were reading at the state proficiency level. On average, 56% of the students in the sample of schools were reading at their state's proficiency level.

In order to maintain the anonymity of schools, schools were assigned pseudonyms based on the reform with which they were working and the

Table A.1. Demographics of schools in study sample.

School	*State*	*Urbanicity*	*At Standard in Reading (%)*	*School Size (number of students)*	*Receiving Free or Reduced-Price Lunch (%)*	*Black (%)*	*Hispanic (%)*
FTF1	PA	Urban fringe	53	1904	33	46	8
FTF2	LA	Large city	9	1470	51	99	0
FTF3	TX	Large city	53	2164	86	11	79
HSTW1	IA	Mid-sized city	50	1142	35	22	4
HSTW2	GA	Rural	92	1436	25	1	2
HSTW3	NJ	Urban fringe	95	575	NA	5	3
SN1	PA	Large city	14	1150	91	47	6
SN2	TX	Urban fringe	71	4778	35	28	38
SN3	MI	Urban fringe	86	1648	4	0	0
PLN1	PA	Urban fringe	83	1372	0	12	2
PLN2	PA	Urban fringe	83	569	0	0	1
PLN3	NJ	Urban fringe	57	923	37	1	2
RU1	MS	Rural	39	415	99	77	0
RU2	KY	Large city	11	1113	41	50	2
RU3	NY	Mid-sized city	39	478	82	71	25

level of experience they had with that reform. For example, the high school that had just begun working with First Things First at the time of our first visit was labeled FTF1.

DATA COLLECTION

Data were collected for this study over the course of about 28 months. Most early-implementing schools were visited three times, in both the fall and spring of the 2004–05 school year, and again in the spring of 2006. The advanced-implementing schools, or mature sites, were visited in the spring of

2005. Interviews with provider program staff were conducted in the spring of 2005 and again in the fall of 2006. Interviews with district leaders, including any individuals in the central office with responsibility for supporting, coordinating, or overseeing the reform, were conducted at the start of the 2006 calendar year. Most data collection focused on providers, schools, and districts, and occurred at multiple time points and in multiple forms. Each of these data collection activities are described in greater detail below.

School Visits

Preceding each site visit, we conducted phone interviews with either the school's principal or the assistant principal. The purpose of these initial interviews was to introduce the study to the schools, get a sense of the context of the school, gauge the extent of interaction with the provider at that point, and set the groundwork for the upcoming visit.

From October 2004 to January 2005 we visited eight schools that were in either their first or second year of implementation of the improvement program. Due to a delay in securing consent from the provider, the early-implementing SchoolNet schools were visited twice rather than three times, like other early-implementing schools. In February through May 2005 we visited the five mature schools in the sample as well as a first or second visit to the ten early-implementing schools. Finally, we visited the nine early-implementing schools for a second or third time between April and May 2006. One school was closed at the beginning of the second year of the study due to natural disaster. As a result, it was visited only twice. Thus, we conducted three rounds of fieldwork in nine of the ten early-implementing schools, while the mature schools were visited once.

Each visit to a school consisted of two CPRE researchers conducting fieldwork for two days. Data collection during all visits consisted of interviews. Our goal was to conduct up to 24 interviews over the course of the two days. In addition, a survey was administered to staff twice at the early-implementing schools (Spring 2005 and Spring 2006) and once at the mature sites (Spring 2005).

Interview data. For the models that sought to influence the whole school (FTF, HSTW, SN), we interviewed the principal, assistant principals, and subject-matter department chairs, and sought to interview approximately 50% of the core teachers (math, English, history, science), with a maximum of about 24 teachers. For the early-stage implementing schools, our target was to conduct 75% of our interviews with staff members who had direct experience with the reform, with the other 25% being more peripheral to the reform. Where relevant, we also interviewed the reform facilitator or coach. For the reforms that directly involved only a subset of the staff (PLN, RU), we interviewed the principal, assistant principals, subject-matter department chairs, all teachers that were using the reform, plus two additional teachers who were not directly involved in the reform in each of the four core departments. Where relevant, we also interviewed the reform facilitator or coach. Overall, we conducted 384 interviews at the ten early-implementing schools (over the course of three visits) and 83 interviews at the five mature schools. All interviews were digitally recorded and transcribed for subsequent analyses. Table A.2 illustrates the number and timing of interviews at each of the schools.

Separate interview protocols were designed for teachers and school leaders. Teacher protocols requested information about general professional practice, conversation topics and communication patterns in the school, initial exposure to the particular improvement program, and work

Table A.2. School-level interviews.

School	*Round 1 Interviews*	*Round 2 Interviews*	*Round 3 Interviews*	*Total Interviews*	*Total Staff in School*
FTF1	21	18	19	58	160
FTF2	16	11	Closed	27	78
FTF3		14		14	187
HSTW1	16	18	14	48	114
HSTW2	26	16	19	61	115
HSTW3		18		18	60
PLN1	14	13	9	36	61
PLN2	16	11	9	36	73
PLN3		14		14	137
RU1	14	11	6	31	40
RU2	17	11	13	41	157
RU3		16		16	89
SN1		4	10	14	61
SN2		23	9	32	329
SN3		21		21	115
Total	140	219	108	467	

with the program. At the end of the school year, teachers were asked in more detail about their experiences with the improvement program—including trainings, technical assistance, and monitoring. They also were asked about changes that had been made in their schools and classrooms as a result of work with the program, communication with colleagues, and sources of help and advice. Leaders were asked about their roles in selecting, supporting, and monitoring use of the improvement program. They also were asked about interactions with the central office, satisfaction with the reform, and its prospects for sustainability.

During the third visit to early-implementing schools, interview protocols were targeted specifically for each program in order to allow us to collect data about specific practices promoted by the improvement program, in addition to many of the areas above in which we collected longitudinal interview data. For schools that were targeted for intensive leadership studies, interview protocols were developed to capture particular details that had been uncovered during earlier interviews and the first survey administration.

Survey data. As stated above, a survey was administered to school staff in all 15 schools in Spring 2005 and again in early-implementing schools in Spring 2006. We administered our survey in a group setting to all teaching staff. Follow-up surveys were sent to all teachers who did not complete a survey, and lists were sent to administrators seeking their help in order to garner high response rates. The survey requested information about teacher job title, departmental affiliation, primary classroom, and other organizational affiliations. The survey also included a set of questions about teacher attitude about the reform. Finally, the survey collected information about in school communication. Questions were asked about whom respondents sought out for advice about four areas of professional practice: course curriculum and content planning, classroom management, assistance for low-performing students, and the particular improvement program. Data also were collected about friendship connections among staff. Table A.3 below provides response rates for each school in the study at each time point.

Providers

Over the course of 14 months, 25 structured interviews were conducted over the telephone (21) or in person (4) with a total of 18 provider staff members whom we refer to as *provider liaisons*. These individuals were employed by the provider organization and supplied guidance, technical assistance, and general implementation support to teachers, schools, and

Table A.3. Survey response rates.

School	*Round*	*Number of Respondents*	*Total Teachers in School*	*Response Rate*
RU1	1	27	33	0.82
RU1	2	28	36	0.78
RU2	1	66	94	0.70
RU2	2	72	87	0.83
RU3	1	34	50	0.68
FTF1	1	112	136	0.82
FTF1	2	118	136	0.87
FTF2	1	38	60	0.63
FTF3	1	134	151	0.89
HSTW1	1	65	87	0.75
HSTW1	2	61	80	0.76
HSTW2	1	76	94	0.81
HSTW2	2	87	99	0.88
HSTW3	1	53	68	0.78
PLN1	1	60	98	0.61
PLN1	2	59	104	0.57
PLN2	1	46	54	0.85
PLN2	2	46	54	0.85
PLN3	1	82	95	0.86
SN1	1	40	56	0.71
SN1	2	53	62	0.85
SN2	1	165	280	0.59
SN2	2	120	220	0.55
SN3	1	54	88	0.61
Round 1 responses		1052		0.74
Round 2 responses		644		0.77

districts engaged in the reform. The first interviews were conducted prior to CPRE's school-based fieldwork and explored the reform broadly. The second round of interviews were conducted after CPRE researchers had visited the study schools at least once. These conversations with provider liaisons further explored the reform's goals; theories of action, learning, and schooling; and progress in the study schools. The materials collected about the five providers and their reform models varied in quantity and scope. Documents included promotional literature in all cases, and implementation manuals, scheduling guidelines, monitoring tools, and formal evaluations of the reform in some cases.

District

Interviews were conducted with 26 central office staff members, primarily in January 2006. District leaders with responsibility for selecting, supporting, or monitoring the improvement program were targeted for interviews. Staff members were asked to provide a retrospective look at the district prior to the partnership with the improvement program and the motivations for establishing the partnership. They were asked about their understanding of the program, steps they had taken to help it thrive in the district, and ways in which existing district practices had changed or been changed as a result of the partnership with the improvement program.

DATA ANALYSES

The various data sources for this study were analyzed through an iterative process that allowed us to familiarize ourselves with the data, code subsets for various purposes, develop and test hypotheses, advance and adjust instruments, and allow themes to emerge.

After each round of fieldwork in the schools, the site visit teams produced a confidential site summary that was organized around initial exploratory themes. These themes included broad categories related to the implementation process, such as contextual factors, experiences with provider, communication within the school, alignment of the provider with other programs/initiatives in the school/district, and staff perceptions of the reform. Site summaries after the second round of fieldwork in the spring of 2005 were expanded to include descriptions of leadership, extent of adoption of structure/components of the provider model, obstacles/challenges of implementation, modifications to the provider model, perceived effects of the reform by school faculty, and district role.

Based on analysis and discussion of the site summaries and informed by our continuing explorations of the implementation research, general categories began to emerge as overarching areas for attention:

1. The importance of improvement program design choices
2. Schools' use of the reforms and their perceived effects
3. Within-school communication patterns
4. School leadership
5. The role of the central office

All interview data were divided into these categories and then further coded to capture elements of these areas that had been revealed in the site summaries to be of potential importance. Data then were entered into Atlas.ti, a qualitative data analysis software package, and further coded and analyzed.

In addition, survey data were analyzed. These data were used to analyze individual and organizational characteristics related to communication (further discussed in Chapter 4). In addition, they were analyzed to identify disproportionately influential individuals in each school (further discussed in Chapter 5).

These data were analyzed independently by teams that focused on one of the five categories identified above. Each team developed theoretical frameworks to analyze the data and wrote papers based on their analyses. These papers were presented at an annual meeting of the American Educational Research Association in 2006 where input was gained from fellow researchers. Based on this analysis and feedback, the final round of data collection was modified somewhat. For example, hypotheses about important elements of program design were investigated further with targeted questions at the school and district level as well as in a second round of interviews with provider liaisons. The chapters in this volume represent refinement of our previous thematic work in conjunction with the additional data that followed our earlier analysis. In addition, case studies were developed for each improvement program that participated in the research project. See Chapter 2 for brief descriptions; more detailed case studies can be found on the CPRE website (www.cpre.org).

About the Editors and the Contributors

JOY ANDERSON is a Philadelphia native and a doctoral candidate in Educational Leadership at the University of Pennsylvania's Graduate School of Education. She is a former elementary school teacher who has worked extensively to support the development of partnerships between schools, universities, and community organizations in order to improve both K–16 academic achievement and community life. Her research focuses on models of effective school change, particularly in the areas of curriculum development and professional development for educators. When away from Penn she enjoys singing and touring with an all-female gospel group called Agape.

RUSSELL P. COLE is an Institute of Education Sciences Pre-doctoral Fellow at the University of Pennsylvania, studying Policy Research, Evaluation, and Measurement at the Graduate School of Education. A former high school math teacher, Russell's main field of interest is in quantitative methods, with an emphasis on social network analysis in organizations. Currently, Russell is a research assistant at the Consortium for Policy Research in Education where his dissertation research investigates the impacts of a leadership intervention in Philadelphia elementary schools. He has a master's degree in mathematics education from Teachers College, Columbia University, and a B.A. in computer science from Brown University.

MARGARET E. GOERTZ is Co-director of the Consortium for Policy Research in Education and a Professor of Education Policy in the Graduate School of Education at the University of Pennsylvania. She is a past president of the American Education Finance Association and has been Executive Director of the Education Policy Research Division at the Educational Testing Service. She has published widely on standards-based accountability. Her current research interests include education finance, education policy, and intergovernmental relations, with particular attention to fiscal and programmatic equity.

MATTHEW GOLDWASSER is an independent educational consultant and ethnographer who specializes in research and evaluation of high schools and high school reform models. Matthew earned his Ph.D. from the University of Colorado at Boulder.

KATHERINE H. HOVDE is an independent consultant with over 15 years of experience in the design, implementation, and evaluation of education policies and programs in the United States and internationally. She has worked extensively for the World Bank and, previously, for the Consortium for Policy Research in Education on an evaluation of the National Center for Education and the Economy's America's Choice comprehensive educational reform package. She holds a master's degree in international affairs from Columbia University.

DIANE MASSELL is a Senior Researcher at the Consortium for Policy Research in Education at the University of Michigan, Ann Arbor. Her research focuses on the relationship between federal, state, and district policy and schooling practices. She received her Ph.D. from Stanford University.

JENNIFER A. MUELLER is a former researcher at the Consortium for Policy Research in Education at the University of Pennsylvania, where her work focused on high school improvement and the use of data in instructional improvement efforts. Jennifer holds a B.S. from Indiana University and an M.S.Ed. from the University of Pennsylvania. She is currently in law school at the University of Illinois.

MATTHEW RIGGAN is a CPRE researcher at the University of Pennsylvania. He earned his Ph.D. at Penn, where his research focused on evaluation strategies for collaborative, community-based programs. Before joining CPRE in 2002, he spent five years developing service learning, after-school, youth development, and adult education programs in West Philadelphia public schools. His current research interests include informal and distributed leadership and organizational learning in schools.

CATHERINE DUNN SHIFFMAN is an Assistant Professor at Shenandoah University and a former researcher at CPRE. She holds a Ph.D. in education policy from Vanderbilt University, an Ed.M. from the Harvard Graduate School of Education, and a B.A. from Middlebury College. Her research interests include school reform, the intersection of education and social policies for families living in poverty, and family–school–community relations.

JONATHAN A. SUPOVITZ (Editor) is an Associate Professor in the Graduate School of Education at the University of Pennsylvania and a Senior Researcher in the Consortium for Policy Research in Education (CPRE). He is the principal investigator or co-principal investigator of several research and evaluation projects at CPRE, including the Study of High School Strategies for Instructional Improvement, the national evaluation of the America's Choice comprehensive school reform design, and an experimental evaluation of a principal leadership development initiative. His research focuses on organizational support for the improvement of teaching and learning through a variety of means. He has written extensively on district support for instructional improvement, educational leadership, and data use.

ELLIOT H. WEINBAUM (Editor) is a Research Assistant Professor at the University of Pennsylvania's Graduate School of Education and a Senior Researcher at the Consortium for Policy Research in Education. His work there focuses on the development of education policy and its impact on practice and improvement at the high school and central office levels. His research interests include intergovernmental relations, performance-based accountability, and high school improvement efforts. Recent research projects and publications include an investigation of the influence of performance-based accountability systems on central office function, a longitudinal look at the impact of state policy, and an analysis of the origins and impacts of the intergovernmental system on education policy. Elliot is a graduate of the Philadelphia public schools and holds a B.A. from Yale University and a Ph.D. from the University of Pennsylvania.

MICHAEL J. WEISS is a graduate student and an Institute of Education Sciences Pre-doctoral Fellow at the University of Pennsylvania's Graduate School of Education studying educational policy. After earning his master's degree in applied statistics at Cornell University, he worked as a data analyst at the Educational Testing Service. His current research includes measuring school performance as it relates to No Child Left Behind and an evaluation of the federal growth-model pilot program. His main fields of interest are value-added modeling, growth models, randomized controlled trials, school finance, and social network analysis.

Index